ABBA ISN'T
DADDY

and Other
BIBLICAL
SURPRISES

"Fr. Burton takes delight in unpacking scripture and making it relevant and approachable. *Abba Isn't Daddy and Other Biblical Surprises* describes the basic tools of Catholic scripture study—then puts them to work on some surprising common misconceptions about the Bible."

Sarah Christmyer
Author, codeveloper, and founding editor of The Great Adventure
Catholic Bible Study

"The Bible is the most important thing a Christian can read. But relying on assumptions about the Bible, or attempting to interpret it for oneself, is the kind of dangerous game that has splintered and politicized Christianity over the centuries. Fr. Burton dispels common myths and misconceptions about scripture while holding it in the highest regard, and shows why Christians should read and study the Bible while also relying on the wisdom of magisterial scholarship to understand what it means. Offering his own thoughts and questions in continuity with time-tested scholarly interpretations, Fr. Burton encourages readers to think of the Bible as more than some display item on a bookshelf, but rather as a key to understanding the ongoing drama of God's love for his people."

Matt Swaim
Communications coordinator for the Coming Home Network
Cohost of the *Son Rise Morning Show*

"If you love how scripture can surprise and bewilder you all at the same time, you need to read Fr. William Burton's book. Burton is gifted in his ability to 'translate' passages that may confuse and open new ways for our understanding and wonder. This book will be an asset for individuals who want to deepen their relationship with God's Word, for adult faith-sharing groups as well as group Bible study. Burton's scholarship and humor make the Bible come alive and connect with Jesus' disciples today calling them to avoid trying to tame the scriptures and instead enjoy the surprises God has in store."

Catherine Sims
Associate director of the Institute for Lay Formation
University of Saint Mary of the Lake

"It is no surprise that Fr. William Burton can enlighten and entertain even the most knowledgeable Bible scholars. Beginning with his introduction that we are the beloved of God, he creates a desire to study, reflect, question, and further understand our own Church history. Reading Burton's words was a long-awaited and joyous voyage I had been meaning to endeavor. I suggest that everyone go and do likewise."

Jan C. Pedroza
Religious Education Congress program coordinator and
early childhood faith formation coordinator
Archdiocese of Los Angeles

"Fr. William Burton writes clearly, authoritatively, and lovingly. Insight-generating examples flow through his text. Teachers, students, and lay study groups will enjoy and learn much from this marvelous work."

Fr. Robert J. Karris, O.F.M.
Professor emeritus at St. Bonaventure University
Former president of the Catholic Biblical Association of America

"*Abba Isn't Daddy and Other Biblical Surprises* offers a clear understanding of contemporary biblical scholarship for thoughtful and interested Catholics who want to learn more about the Bible, but don't have the time to study Greek and Hebrew. Thoroughly grounded in Church documents, it offers new and surprising insights on familiar Bible passages that will deepen your understanding and appreciation of God's holy Word."

Mary Elizabeth Sperry
Author of *Bible Top Tens* and *Scripture in the Parish*

"Fr. Burton offers lovely gems in each chapter of this scripture mine, and by the end he has flipped over an ordinary lump of stone to uncover an enormous glittering jewel that you get to keep!"

Sonja Corbitt
Host of *Bible Study Evangelista* and author of *Unleashed* and *Fearless*

ABBA ISN'T DADDY

and other BIBLICAL SURPRISES

What Catholics Really Need to Know about Scripture Study

◄ William L. Burton, O.F.M. ►

AVE MARIA PRESS AVE Notre Dame, Indiana

Contents

PART I

Scripture Scholarship:
LET'S LEARN SOME BASICS!

The Bible is filled with surprises!

By the time you finish reading this book, you will find this statement to be very true. Here's another statement: studying the Bible is itself a fun and entertaining endeavor. Now, you may not be so sure of this one! In fact, many Catholics are intimidated by Bible study. They shy away from it, thinking it to be "too hard" or something reserved for experts and priests. This isn't so! You really can study the Bible and find it to be an engaging and fun experience. Stay with me! You *will* be surprised!

Let me first point out that some of the revelations you will read about in this book won't be surprising to you now, but they once were. For example, you probably know that Jesus is known as "Jesus Christ" in the New Testament but that Christ is *not* his last name. You likely also know that the Bible was not recorded in "real time"; that is, there were not people following Jesus and recording his words as he spoke. There was no "on site" journalist reporting on the Exodus. The material in the Bible—in both the Old Testament and the New Testament (except for the New Testament letters)—was written well after the events that the writers described. But even if you already knew these facts, there is more to each of these lessons that will indeed surprise you.

1

On the other hand, this book does contain even more information that you will read about for the first time. You know that Jesus called God "Father." Have you also heard that Jesus was the first to do so? Is this really true? The word Jesus used for Father was *abba*. Has someone told you that Abba translates to a very familiar term for Father, like "Daddy"? Is this true, too, or not? When Jesus was asked by his disciples to teach them a prayer, he led them in one that begins with the words "Our Father." This is the well-known Lord's Prayer. You likely have assumed that the words of this prayer were never recited before Jesus spoke them. But is this also true? You may be surprised at the answers to these and other questions.

For most of my life, I've been praying and studying scripture and have found among its pages endless surprises. Some of the surprises are small, some are big—huge, actually—and all are fascinating. Some of these scriptural surprises are readily understood; others are more complex and demand careful scrutiny—but all of them are inspiring and enriching.

In this book, we'll look at some of these biblical surprises, focusing on the life of Jesus. But before we do, in part I, we'll examine some of the basics of scripture scholarship. We'll look at how the Catholic Church has wisely and carefully approved of scripture study. We'll explain what it means to say that "the Bible is true" and "the Bible is without error." We'll introduce the principle methods of scripture scholarship. We'll take a fascinating look at the important role that Israel's location and geography played in creating the Bible, especially in the country's proximity to Egypt. We'll examine the mechanics of recording the Bible, and the high monetary cost of producing ancient Bibles. We'll explain how and why divisions—chapters and verses—were added to the Bible. In your reading of this book, it's wise and necessary to have a Bible handy for the journey—preferably, but not necessarily, a *New American Bible, Revised Edition*.

Let's move forward!

≺ 1 ≻

Our Loving God Is the Subject of the Bible

God himself is a God of surprises. Everything we know about God demonstrates that this is so. Right from the very beginning, at the time of creation, this is clear. Creation itself is a surprise. God didn't need to create anything at all. God is totally self-sufficient, in want of nothing. Yet, "God so loved the world . . ." that a beloved *had* to be created—the object of God's love that could, didn't have to, but *could* respond freely to the love God offered. So the universe was formed and a planet within it was created with a garden that would provide the beloved with an all-supplying home. On this planet with a garden, we, the beloved of God, would find all that was needed to give and sustain our lives. It really is amazing to think that the eternal God began time so that we creatures could be *inserted into* time. God had no need to do any of this but he did it. Why?

It was love that compelled God to create and his love is built into and evident in all of creation. We are the objects of divine love. A relationship of love demands the consent of the beloved, the partnership of the beloved, and the cooperation of the beloved, and this response of love must be freely chosen. Love demands free interaction; it cannot be coerced. Love must come from free will. It is from this surprising initiative of God that all creation comes. What a surprise this all is!

As Times Goes On

But like any surprise that repeats itself, the initial impact can wear off. We often forget how amazing it is that this world consistently gives us all that we need. Reimagine what a surprise it is that from a little seed, any seed at all, comes a plant—any and every plant. This plant could be a tuft of grass or a giant two-thousand-year-old sequoia! Looking at that tiny seed, who could ever imagine that from that speck, shoved down into the soil, the largest and oldest living creature could emerge?

This reminds me that when I was a child, my father had the most annoying response to just about anything we kids asked for. It was always the same:

"Dad, can I have a toy fire truck?"

"Whaddya think these toys grow on trees?"

Or, "Dad, can I have a chemistry kit?"

"Whaddya think these kits grow on trees?"

However, "Dad, can I have an apple?"

"Whaddya think these apples grow on . . ." Oops!

Just imagine, God has designed a garden for us to live in and within this garden God created and placed leafy creatures, fruit trees that literally push food out to us on the ends of tree limbs! Again, because we are so accustomed to it, the surprising phenomenon of fruit-bearing trees goes all but unnoticed. Yet it is really a stunning surprise. How could we ever imagine that from the woody "stuff" of a tree limb, edible, delicious fruit could emerge? How is it that potatoes can come up from the sandy soil? How can sweet grapes emerge from a vine? And that huge watermelons grow from that spindly little stem? Who could know that soil, rain, and a seed can conspire to produce a flower, a fruit, a vegetable, or a leafy shade tree?

The surprising love of God surrounds us, gives us life, and supports our very existence. We are swimming in the nourishing waters of divine love. But like the fish unaware of the water in which it swims, so we, God's most beloved creatures, are too often unaware of the divine love that envelops us. Yet if we can step back and look at it, we can see that we are the beneficiaries of a benevolence that is without reason. It is a love that is surprisingly uncalled for. Yet here we all are, living in the midst of an all-providing garden.

The ultimate surprise of love is that God wished to share completely in the life we have been given. So God began to reveal his divine self to us. In giving us minds to perceive creation, we learned of the Creator. We learned the logic of God. In nature, we studied the science of God. We began to recognize the beauty of God. We perceived that God is a loving God.

In our hearts that God made, his voice stirs. These stirrings teach us how to live with one another. In tablets that came from the place of the shocking flaming bush, God tried to teach us how to share this earthly home with one another. We fail more often than we learn. But surprisingly, God tries again and again; in other ways, in various hearts, stirred by loving urges, God tries to teach us. With stunning patience, God repeatedly tries to reveal himself to us.

These revelations of God were eventually recorded in sacred writings and collected in a book we now call the Bible. The big surprise of the Old Testament is that God chose a particular people to reveal himself to: slaves he rescued from bondage in Egypt, the Hebrews who became known as Jews. It wasn't only the choice of a particular people that was surprising; it was the way God organized them and had them relate to one another and to him.

God Reveals More of Himself

All ancient religions of the Near East reinforced the sociopolitical status quo of human society. In other words, the hierarchy of the gods within their pantheons represented a heavenly version of the sociopolitical hierarchies of their earthly societies. In those ancient religions, there was a celestial pyramid of authority and honor among the gods. The "boss" god was always on top. That authority and honor then cascaded down to each lower rung of the pyramid to the lowest heavenly beings and certainly to the lowest rung of all, human beings. Tasks of the gods were distributed among them that marked or sustained their status within the pyramid of the pantheon. There may have been a god of the sea, a god of the sun, and many other gods charged with certain elements of the world.

In earthly societies of the time, human and religious structures mirrored each other. The head of state, usually the monarch, ruled with divine authority over the other members of the royal family or his tribe. The honor and respect due the monarch diffused down throughout the hierarchical levels of society with marked roles or expectations distributed among each social level, from the highest levels of social honor (and usually wealth) down through to the lowest level. This was the level usually occupied by slaves. This infusion of religious meaning into the social structure provided "divine" authority to support and reinforce the sociopolitical hierarchical status quo on earth.

And yet among the Hebrews of the Old Testament, God surprisingly entered into human history to turn this hierarchical pyramid on its head. The book of Exodus records God taking the part of slaves—the bottom rung of the social ladder—against their masters. And note, the master of these slaves was none other than the most powerful human being of ancient history, the pharaoh of Egypt! Talk about a surprise! God takes the part of slaves not just to defend them from the highest level of social power, but to defeat the power of the pharaoh so that these slaves could be free and find a home among the nations of the world. This is shocking! Gods are supposed to reinforce the social structure, not upend it!

This surprising nature of God and how he relates to his people is noted again and again in the Bible. For example:

> Ask now of the days of old, before your time, ever
> since God created humankind upon the earth; ask

> from one end of the sky to the other: Did anything so great ever happen before? Was it ever heard of? Did a people ever hear the voice of God speaking from the midst of fire, as you did, and live? Or did any god venture to go and take a nation for himself from the midst of another nation, by testings, by signs and wonders, by war, with strong hand and outstretched arm, and by great terrors, all of which the LORD, your God, did for you in Egypt before your very eyes? All this you were allowed to see that you might know that the LORD is God; there is no other. (Dt 4:32–35)

Like all lovers who wish to share deeply and intimately in the life of the beloved, so too with God. So the Divine Word would clothe itself in the flesh and life of a man. The ineffable, unspeakable God was spoken in humanity as the Christ. The almighty became the defenseless, the needy baby of Mary. In this Word of flesh and blood, God sought to speak plainly and clearly to us. He strove to communicate to us the all-surprising divine love. The love that was Jesus of Nazareth would then confront our sinfulness and, without flinching, experience other dark aspects of human life: hate, pain, disillusionment, heartbreak. As St. Francis of Assisi put it, "Love was not loved." Sadly, this pain, too, is part of the experience of God's beloved children, a part that God, surprisingly, also shared.

The followers of Jesus shared memories of their experience of this love-made-man. Eventually those memories of what Jesus taught and how he lived were recorded. The Word of God was scratched in black blood ink onto papyrus and parchment. So it should not surprise us that the written record of God's love should itself be filled with many surprises as well.

⤙ 2 ⤚

What Is the Bible?

When I was a young layman, twenty-six years old, living in Philadelphia, working for a brokerage service company, I got an awful telephone call from my family telling me that my father had died. Then nine months later, the same thing happened. I received a call that my mother had died. My family was far away from me, in the Midwest. While my dad had been sick with a negative prognosis of lung cancer, he'd lived six months longer than his doctor had predicted. So while it was jarring to get that call, it was not unexpected. But my mother's death was a terrible shock. While my brothers and sisters and I had been concerned about how she'd fare after Dad's death, we were happily surprised to watch her come through the initial grief and begin to do things like make house improvements and start volunteer work. We all said to ourselves, "She's gonna make it." So when I received notice of her death, I was stunned. It was truly awful news.

My father was fifty-eight when he died, and my mom was fifty-nine. At the time, I thought this was much too young for them to have been taken from me. After their deaths, I began to feel a kind of resentment—completely inexplicable to me—toward older people. In fact, I specifically recall riding my bike along the Kelly Drive bike path in Philadelphia. I noticed a woman riding nearby who looked to be about sixty-five or seventy years old. And I thought, "Why is she still alive and healthy and my mother, several years younger, not?" I'm ashamed to admit that this happened often and the more it did, the angrier I got about my parents' deaths. What kept coming back to me was the verbal equivalent of a fist shaking in protest against the sky: "This isn't fair!"

Five years later, almost to the month of my mother's death, I got what felt like a blinding insight about my anger and resentment. My father had always been a very active, even athletic man. He could ride bicycles backward! (Don't ask me how.) I had seen him walk on his hands at age fifty, up and down the banked lawn of our neighbor's front yard, just to get our five-year-old neighbor to giggle. My father was a construction worker for thirty-three years, and that work meant he was regularly climbing ladders and walking on scaffolding. He even perched occasionally in a boatswain chair to reach work areas high above the ground. My mom wasn't athletic by any stretch, but she certainly was active. No mother of five children, each thirteen months apart, could *not* be active and a hard worker.

Then I began to imagine my parents as really old people. And I realized that both of them would not have "aged gracefully." The challenges and vagaries of old age would have likely been terrible burdens for them. Imagining the scene of my dad's movement being limited by an oxygen tube attached to a tank was one of tragedy for me. I knew my dad could not have tolerated the limitations that advanced years and deteriorating health would have imposed on him. The same was true for my mom. She would have had great difficulty resigning herself to years of incapacitation and a shrinking circle of activity.

And what about us kids? How hard would it have been for us to watch our lively, energetic parents diminish? We would have struggled watching our active parents grow older. It would have taken its toll on us as well. I would have hated to see them in such circumstances.

So I began to see—and I know this sounds odd—that their relatively early deaths were in some ways, really, a blessing. What had appeared to me as an unfair tragedy, a source of pain and anger in me five years before, I now began to see as a grace from God. Yes, a blessing.

Looking back on my experience became a theological reflection on how God had been working in my life and in the lives of my folks. I didn't see it at the time, in the shock of their deaths, but it was in that theological reflection later that I began to see the hand of God at work. I saw God's care, mercy, and great compassion both for my parents and for me and my brothers and sisters. Theologically reflecting on my past, I saw God working. I did not see his hand when I was in the exact moment of the experience, but I could clearly see that he had been at work when I reviewed my own and my family's history five years after the fact.

The Bible Is a Theological Reflection Too!

The type of experience I had reflecting on my parents' deaths years later and finding God's presence is a similar dynamic to that which took place in the creation of both the Old Testament and New Testament of sacred scripture. The Bible is the record of the theological reflections of the people of God on their own history and experience. They began to understand more about God in terms of their later reflections on their history. It was in those reflections that they came to see the hand of God at work. This tells us something important about what the Bible is and is not. The Bible is a theological reflection on history and how, in that reflection, the people of God began to see God working in their lives. The Bible is *not* a history book. This is clear when we look at *both* the Old Testament and the New Testament.

We find no written eyewitness accounts of events in the Old Testament or of the events in the Gospels. No one was recording a diary of the events of Israel's history as they happened. There was no one reporting on the activity and speeches of Jesus as they occurred. Rather, in the Old Testament, we find a record of what the Jews told and retold one another of their history. For centuries, the Jews orally passed on their traditions about their past, generation to generation, each retelling shaped by further and deeper reflection. Likewise, the eyewitnesses of Jesus handed down their stories and memories of Jesus orally; only a later generation would attempt to record the stories and memories that had been told to them. In the process of handing down oral accounts, those who shared the accounts added theological reflections about how they saw and understood God at work in their history.

Eventually, God-inspired authors began to write down the traditional accounts that they'd heard and retold. Even these earliest written accounts would be edited and rewritten as the authors' theological insights into their past deepened and broadened. Succeeding editors of the sacred texts would also make changes in the accounts to reflect the situations at the time of that writer or editor.

Let me give an example from the Old Testament. The book of Daniel purports to be an account of the events of the terrible Babylonian crisis. This crisis, which occurred in the sixth century BC, culminated in the destruction of the first Temple and the city of Jerusalem by Nebuchadnezzar. But in fact, the book of Daniel was written not in the sixth century BC but actually four hundred years later, in the second century BC. It was not written in the time of the Babylonian persecution and exile but during a later crisis of the persecution and occupation of Jerusalem by the Greek king of the Seleucid Empire, Antiochus Epiphanes IV.

Antiochus Epiphanes IV, this later persecutor and destroyer of Jerusalem, dominated Israel during the Hellenistic period, a time of subjugation by Greek rulers whose dynasties were descendants of Alexander the Great's surviving generals. The crisis stirred up by Antiochus in Jerusalem was both military and religious in nature. He had been trying to conquer Egypt, then ruled by another Hellenistic king of the Greek Ptolemaic dynasty, Ptolemy VI. Antiochus's military adventure in 169 BC against Ptolemy VI failed. The people living in Jerusalem—Jews and Gentiles alike—knew of this defeat. A rumor also spread in Israel that Antiochus had been killed. This sparked an uprising by some of the Jewish residents of Jerusalem.

Worried that the Roman overlords would see this Jewish uprising as a sign of his weakness, Antiochus tried to squash this rebellion as quickly and as ruthlessly as possible. He issued orders that the Jewish religion was illegal and was to be extinguished. Within this terrible persecution of the Jews, Antiochus captured the rebuilt Temple in Jerusalem and erected statues of pagan gods inside the Temple. This was the "abomination of desolation" that would fire up the Jewish Maccabean family to organize a military revolt.

The author of the book of Daniel wrote in the second century BC, during the dangerous and calamitous time of Antiochus IV's persecutions of the Jews. Yet the author purports to be writing during the earlier sixth century BC in order to make obvious parallels between the Babylonian king, Nebuchadnezzar, and Antiochus Epiphanes IV. Just as Nebuchadnezzar had destroyed the first Temple, so Antiochus had spiritually destroyed the second Temple with his abominable idolatry. The persecutions by Antiochus that occurred during the time of writing (second century BC) profoundly affected how the author of Daniel wrote about the past (sixth century BC). Reflection on the past tragedy of the Babylonian crisis produced insights that would help the author of the book of Daniel explain how God continued to work in the history of the Chosen People in the *current* crisis of the Jews under Antiochus Epiphanes IV.

Another example comes from the book of Isaiah. This prophetic book was actually made up of material that was written at different times and by different authors. Chapters 1–39 were written during the Assyrian crisis of the eighth century BC, while chapters 40–55 were written by a different author during the Babylonian crisis, some 150 years later. If we don't understand that the first thirty-nine chapters were addressed to Jews during the Assyrian crisis and the second part was written to Jews during that later catastrophe of the Babylonian exile, then we will misinterpret the message of each. Needless to say, the prophet writing the second part of the book of Isaiah benefitted from the first author's theological reflection on the earlier Assyrian crisis. This reflection helped him to address his contemporaries facing the catastrophe of the Babylonian exile and subsequent destruction of the Temple in Jerusalem.

Understanding this view of the overall process of the formation of the biblical texts (event, reflection, writing) will help us not only to accurately interpret them but, just as importantly, to appreciate the great complexities involved in the study and interpretation of scripture. It is this very complexity that demands the guidelines and processes provided by Church tradition and teaching in regard to sacred scripture.

The Bible Comes from the Church!

The heading of this subsection points to a necessary truth. Sacred scripture is the speech of God written under the inspiration of the Holy Spirit. The task of interpreting authentically the Word of God falls to the Church, particularly the Church's Magisterium. This makes sense. Who of us individually has the time or the particular talents needed for the dedication to such tasks? Individually none of us could become experts in all of the scholarly fields that would be needed in order to speak with any expert authority on the vast array of biblical topics. But it is not only the complexity and technical challenges presented by these ancient texts that demand the help of the Church.

The Bible as we have it today emerged *from* the Church! The Church not only incorporated books of the Jewish or Hebrew

Bible into the canon of what came to be called the Old Testament, but early members of the Church were the authors of the books of the New Testament! The apostles and their successors guided early Christians in their understanding of God's Revelation to Israel (the Old Testament) in terms of the Revelation in Christ (the New Testament) from within an already established community of faith.

St. Paul's letters and Acts of the Apostles witness clearly that there were already several well-established Christian communities scattered around and throughout the Mediterranean who were already celebrating the Eucharist on a weekly basis as well as baptizing new members. These early church communities were up and running, establishing liturgical practice, and assembling internal structures of authority among themselves all before even the first Gospel account was written (the Gospel of Mark, ca. AD 66). There was a Church before there was a New Testament!

Christ's teaching both by words and by example was handed down within the Church from the first companions of Jesus, the apostles. This was done primarily by simply talking—telling and retelling stories and memories of Jesus to any who would listen. Then later, the record of Christians who had not been eyewitnesses of Christ but who were the eyewitnesses of the apostles was written down. It is this second and even third generation of Christians then who would write the books of the New Testament. As the texts were assembled, the gospels took a place of primacy in the New Testament.

Within the New Testament itself, especially in the Pauline and other letters, we see early Christian writers interpreting Jesus' life and words for the early Church. Immediately after the compilation of the New Testament books, early commentators and bishops sought to convey Christ's life and teaching to the people of that post-apostolic time. The Church was spreading far and wide throughout the Roman Empire. Gentiles were swelling the ranks of the new movement. Questions that the apostles never had to face were confronting the young Church and her teachers—questions that had to be answered. So these early teachers of the Church had to find ways to speak to new people and new situations—ways that were still faithful to what Christ taught his apostles and to what God had revealed.

I stress this historical timeline because understanding this makes it easier to see how and why the Church has authority when it comes to interpreting, explaining, and handing on the biblical texts.

The Nature of Roman Catholic Teaching on the Bible

It is necessary to state at the outset that trying to press the two-thousand-year history of Roman Catholic teaching concerning the Bible into a single chapter is a fool's errand. Can't be done. It is impossible because the Church has had so much to say over the past twenty centuries about the Bible and how to study the Bible. We will proceed, ever mindful of the Church's directions on biblical study, using the most important and recent official teachings of the Church to guide us.

Most of the documents we're going to look at for Church teaching in the areas of the Bible and biblical study are encyclical letters. These types of letters are very similar in purpose and style to the ones St. Paul wrote to early Church communities and that are included in the New Testament. Encyclical letters are forms of communicating theological and pastoral teaching to the Church. There are also other official instructions issued that are called apostolic letters, or pastoral letters.

Interestingly, just as the authors of the books of the Bible relied on the previous theological reflections of those who passed on the sacred accounts, the teaching authorities of the Church today (the pope and bishops) always connect a "current teaching" to what was taught by the Church in the past. This is why almost all magisterial documents consistently look backward to previous Church documents, papal letters, revered theologians, and the like to show how current teaching is consistent with earlier tradition and teaching. This is done even though the current audience and circumstances being addressed are different from those audiences and circumstances of the past.

A good example is the last encyclical issued by Pope St. John XXIII, *Pacem in Terris* (*Peace on Earth*). In this letter, he cites the previous teachings of his predecessors, Pope Leo XIII, Pope Pius XII, and others, and yet he speaks to the crisis that was threatening world peace at the time that he wrote. The "current world" for Pope St. John XXIII was the 1963 Cold War world, just after the frightening Cuban missile crisis and a mere eighteen years after the atomic bombings of Hiroshima and Nagasaki. This was certainly *not* the world of the apostles, nor even the world of the pope's predecessors. It was a world that those of the past could not even have imagined. But this is how the Church operates. She applies the consistent teachings of the past to those circumstances and realities of the present and the foreseeable future. The same method applies to how the Church teaches about the Bible and how to study the Bible.

As you will see when we look at Church teaching concerning the Bible, each document looks both to the past and to the present circumstances. Certainly no pope or Church authority can contradict past teaching but is obliged to apply such teaching to the present. (This will be particularly clear in the discussion of Pope Pius XII's encyclical *Divino Afflante Spiritu*.) As you can imagine, being faithful to past teaching while applying its lessons to the present is not always easy. The realities of the present and the Catholics of the present, the whole world of the present, are in many ways vastly different from the realities of the contexts of past Church teachings.

≺ 3 ≻

How Does the Church Study the Bible?

To learn more about what the Church teaches about the Bible and biblical studies, let's begin as most would expect when looking at Church teaching: with the *Catechism of the Catholic Church*. In Part One of the *Catechism*, you will find thirty-three paragraphs (101–133) that deal particularly with sacred scripture. These paragraphs speak in mostly general terms about the Bible.

You will notice immediately that the paragraphs are comprised mainly of references to prior magisterial documents of the Church, especially *Dei Verbum* (*DV*) (*Word of God*) from the Second Vatican Council. The conciliar constitution *Dei Verbum* is cited some twenty-seven times within these thirty-three paragraphs of the *Catechism*. At first glance, this may seem like overreliance on one reference. However, we must remember that the most authoritative magisterial instruments in the Catholic Church are the documents that originate from ecumenical councils. So it makes sense that the *Catechism* privileges the teachings promulgated by the most recent ecumenical council, the Second Vatican Council, which took place from 1962 to 1965.

To reach a more detailed and pertinent Church teaching concerning the Bible and biblical studies, we really have to get to the more focused magisterial teachings of the last century or so that have been issued in the form of papal encyclicals and declarations of the Pontifical Biblical Commission (PBC). The PBC serves as a papal "committee of experts," convened at the desire of the pope to study particular issues concerning Church teachings about the Bible. The findings of the PBC are usually published under the signature of both the pope and the *ex officio* chairman of the commission, the head of the Congregation for the Doctrine of Faith.

There are two sources I recommend for anyone interested in having the Church's recent magisterial documents on the Bible collected in one volume: *The Bible Documents: A Parish Resource with Commentary and Index*[1] and Daniel Harrington's *Witnesses to the Word: New Testament Studies since Vatican II.*[2] While these are both excellent resources, the Harrington volume offers a more up-to-date survey of scholarly advances in New Testament study.

A Short History of Modern Biblical Scholarship

My years of biblical study have shown me that one outstanding feature of Church teaching on biblical studies is that the Church's approach is a reasonable one. By that I mean that even if one were not a Catholic or even not a believer at all, any thinking person could see that the Church has proceeded logically, fairly, and with academic rigor on this topic.

This light of logic shines most brightly in the past century or more. In the mid-1800s, major archeological and linguistic studies were beginning to surface from the nations and cultures of the Ancient Near East. From Mesopotamia to Egypt, the secrets of the past were starting to be unlocked as long-buried stones of past cities began to tell their stories to archeologists and scholars began to decipher languages long forgotten.

All of us live in a time when the sacred writing of ancient Egypt—called *hieroglyphics*—is well known, at least by experts. So in our present day, it can be difficult to appreciate the fact that the voices of ancient Egypt had been mute until the successful deciphering of hieroglyphics in 1822 by Frenchman Jean-François Champollion from the famous Rosetta Stone. Until that time, people didn't know what those curious symbols and ideographs meant. With the discovery of this key, the whole world of ancient Egypt opened up to scholars.

Further east, in the lands of Mesopotamia, later discoveries and linguistic work also gave voice to the once-mute cultures of ancient Assyria, Babylonia, Persia, and many others that were in close proximity to Israel and, by this connection, close to the events described in the Bible and to the formation of the Bible itself. The deciphering of thousands of cuneiform tablets and inscriptions that began in the mid-1800s translated several languages used by these cultures. Using the cuneiform tablets and inscriptions, scholars could then compare non-Jewish and non-Christian "witnesses" to much of the scope of biblical history. For the first time in modern history, we had perspectives on biblical times that were written from the point of view of contemporary, non-biblical sources.

These discoveries revealed that the cultures neighboring Israel were very similar to Israel. And not only that—the religion of Judaism and the religions of many surrounding nations were also alike in many ways. For example, we learned that much of the literature of the Bible was similar to—if not downright borrowed from—the cultures in and around ancient Palestine. Stories similar to the great flood from Genesis 6:5–7:22 and those about the patriarch Joseph (Gn 37ff.) were found in Ancient Near Eastern literature, which predated the biblical texts. Some of the biblical wisdom literature once thought to be peculiar to ancient Judaism was found to have similarly existed in Egypt and Babylonia. Other newly discovered texts described the same battles found in the Old Testament but written from the perspective of Israel's opponents. You can imagine both the excitement and confusion that these discoveries caused. In short, the more we learned, the more we learned!

These exciting discoveries started a great, renewed debate among Catholic biblical scholars and scholars from other Christian denominations as well, concerning how best to understand scripture in the light of this new information. Much of the astounding information that was coming from the Ancient Near East in the late nineteenth century was catalogued and recorded by German Protestant scholars. They began composing dictionaries (lexica) and grammar rules of these once-lost languages to aid them translating and understanding the Hebrew and Aramaic languages that were used in the Bible. Already by this time, the Catholic Church saw that her own biblical scholarship had to "catch up" with the Protestant scholars in finding ways to integrate these new discoveries and guide their use in researching and studying the Bible.

The Church Responds with Documents That Address Biblical Scholarship and Study

These archaeological, linguistic, and historical discoveries raised serious questions about the understanding of biblical texts. Some of these questions seemed to threaten both Church teaching and personal faith. Catholic scholars were not always sure what to make of some of these scholarly advances. Furthermore, since much of this new scholarship was dominated by non-Catholic scholars, these Protestant scholars occasionally interpreted their findings to contradict or at least cast doubt on Church teaching. And Catholic teaching was not alone in being questioned. Many Protestant churches found their views of scripture being shaken as a result of much of the new scholarship emerging from the late 1800s and early 1900s.

How did the Catholic Church respond? Primarily through a series of encyclicals and other magisterial documents mainly intended to direct academic biblical scholarship. Each of these documents helped Catholic scholars advance their understanding and improve their ability to correctly interpret scripture. For general information, in the sections that follow I will refer in detail to two Church documents regarding biblical studies: *Providentissimus Deus* and *Divino Afflante Spiritu*. They are monumental among other significant documents produced since the late nineteenth century, many by the Pontifical Biblical Commission.

Providentissimus Deus (*On the Study of Holy Scripture*) (1893)

Providentissimus Deus (*PD*) is an encyclical written by Pope Leo XIII. (This is the same pope who wrote the famous hallmark document on Church social teaching, *Rerum Novarum*.) *Providentissimus Deus* focuses primarily on the preparation and proper dispositions of professors of scripture for seminaries and academic institutions.

While Pope Leo was at pains to praise the traditional approaches of scripture study, including "the tradition of antiquity" that focuses on the official Vulgate Latin edition of the Bible, later in the encyclical he encourages the study of "other (biblical) versions of Christian antiquity," that is, the original Hebrew and Greek versions of the Bible. To support this directive he quotes both St. Augustine and, notably, St. Jerome, who wrote that "the office of a commentator [of sacred scripture] is to set forth not what he himself [the commentator] would prefer, but what his author says" (*PD*, 12).

This encyclical also notes that the sciences and theology are separate fields and that the Bible's scope is not scientific in that its concerns do not deal with "the visible world." This suggested to many Catholic biblical scholars of the period that errors of science or history found in the Bible should not be interpreted as a challenge to the truth of the biblical texts. At the same time, this encyclical cautioned scholars about the use of the new methods, what the encyclical calls "higher criticism" (*PD*, 17).

Higher criticism is a term that needs some explanation. What was meant by higher criticism at the time is what is now referred to as the "historical-critical method" (more information to follow in chapter 4). At the turn of the twentieth century, some biblical scholars applied the advances in ancient studies (linguistic, archeological and cultural, etc.) to seriously question the historical truth of the biblical texts. Specifically, the originality of these stories was questioned because, as previously mentioned, so many discoveries revealed that some Ancient Near Eastern narratives were older than the stories in the Bible, yet were so similar to them. It became obvious that many of these ancient stories from neighboring cultures strongly influenced the creation of Old Testament material. This in turn caused many to question how these biblical stories could be "true" or inspired if they were not original.

Typically, the Church had always looked back to Church Fathers—early patristic writers of the third and fourth centuries—as their guides for interpreting scripture. Yet, the ancient Church Fathers were not privy to these later discoveries. What was the Church to make of that? A rationalistic look at the origins of biblical texts demanded a new, modern approach to studying the Bible and questioned the dominance of the patristic approach. The new, higher-critical or historical-critical approach resulted. It focused more on questions of original languages, ancient cultures, and the nature of ancient societies that were oral rather than literate societies.

This new approach stirred deeper tensions within the Catholic Church. Protestant biblical scholarship, particularly in Germany, Britain, and France, raised fundamental questions about how the ancient texts of the Bible were to be studied. Many wanted to study biblical texts using the same new methods with which the ancient texts from other cultures were being studied.

Surprise! Change is hard! Many Catholic scholars feared such approaches would undermine the divine origins and divine authority of biblical texts and resisted studying them the same way contemporary scholars were studying newly discovered Ancient Near East texts. Furthermore, there was a larger challenge to traditional Catholic teaching arising from scholars who were far more secular in their mindset about studying anything and everything. By way of comparison, just think of the challenge that Darwin's discoveries and hypotheses concerning human origins made to the traditional understanding of the book of Genesis.

In fact, secular scholars even questioned the very existence of God and subsequently denied any kind of divine intervention in human history. Needless to say, such secularizing movements, especially in universities, caused the Church to view these developments with skepticism. The Church described this drive toward secularization as "Modernism." In his 1907 encyclical, *Pascendi Dominici Gregis* (*On the Doctrine of the Modernists*), Pope Pius X officially condemned Modernism as heresy. Immediately, this encyclical generated an air of suspicion around the use of the newly discovered methods of biblical inquiry and tainted the new historical-critical method and anyone who used it.

It's no surprise that such an atmosphere put the brakes on Catholic biblical scholarship. Many Catholic professors of the Bible lived in fear that if they were to take up the historical-critical method, they could expose themselves to the accusation of being modernists. An all-or-nothing mentality arose among Catholic biblical scholars. A scholar either eschewed altogether such modern approaches to the Bible or he invited suspicion upon himself. This fear of the charge of Modernism significantly slowed the progress of Catholic scholarship.

In fact, there were many academically sound methods within the historical-critical method that helped to open up once difficult or impenetrable biblical texts. Many thought that these new approaches to the Bible were simply neutral tools for biblical study that did not in any way demand atheism or the denial of any divine truths about God or Church teaching by those who used them. Additionally, scholars soon discovered that careful application of these methods also provided insights into the biblical texts that actually deepened and supported Christian faith. Most Catholic biblical scholars summed up their use of the modern critical tools thus: "Tools are simply tools."

Happily, Pope Pius XII saw the threat in Catholics not being able to use the historical-critical method for study of ancient cultures and languages. In 1943, on the fiftieth anniversary of *Providentissimus Deus*, he produced an encyclical of his own that would encourage Catholic biblical scholars to, in effect, catch up with their Protestant peers.

Divino Afflante Spiritu (*Inspired by the Holy Spirit*) (1943)

Pope Pius XII wrote this encyclical in 1943, during the Second World War and during the occupation of Italy by Germany. For this reason, the full dissemination and appreciation of *Divino Afflante Spiritu* (*DAS*) would be delayed for several years. *Divino Afflante Spiritu* encourages faithfulness to *Providentissimus Deus* and acknowledges the cautions in utilizing the historical-critical method as addressed in *Providentissimus Deus*. Pope Pius XII highlighted a portion of *Providentissimus Deus* and strongly taught that

> it is absolutely wrong and forbidden "either to narrow inspiration to certain passages of Holy Scripture, or to admit that the sacred writer has erred," since

> divine inspiration "not only is essentially incompatible with error but excludes and rejects it as absolutely and necessarily as it is impossible that God Himself, the supreme Truth, can utter that which is not true. This is the ancient and constant faith of the Church." (*DAS*, 3)

Pope Pius XII next, a bit surprisingly, departed from his exclusive endorsement of *Providentissimus Deus* by examining other teachings of Pope Leo XIII on scripture. For example, Pius XII noted that Leo XIII, by his apostolic letter *Vigilantiae* in 1902, established the Pontifical Biblical Commission. Pius cited *Vigilantiae* concerning the responsibilities of the scholars needed to form the commission "whose duty it would be to procure by every means that the sacred texts may receive everywhere among us that more thorough exposition which the times demand, and be kept safe not only from every breath of error, but also from all inconsiderate opinions" (*DAS*, 5).

Pius XII also commended the work of another predecessor, Pope Pius X, for his establishing the Pontifical Biblical Institute (my alma mater!) in 1909. Pius XII quotes Pius X stating that the mission of the institute was to "in the best way possible promote the study of the Bible and *all cognate sciences* in accordance with the mind of the Catholic Church" (*DAS*, 6; emphasis mine). Later in the encyclical, the pope commends the faculty of the Pontifical Biblical Institute. All of this can be viewed as a prelude to the encyclical's encouragement to more openness to modern methods of biblical scholarship for Catholic scholars.

Pope Pius XII exhorted "the biblical scholar" to the study of ancient Hebrew and Greek and "other Oriental languages" and all branches of philology in order "to explain the original text which, having been written by the inspired author himself, has more authority and greater weight than any even the very best translation, . . . this can be done all the more easily and fruitfully, if to the knowledge of languages be joined a real skill in literary criticism of the same text" (*DAS*, 16). All of this study must be done "so as to arrive at a deeper and fuller knowledge of *his* (the biblical writer's) *meaning*" (*DAS*, 15; emphasis mine).

Here it is clear that while holding to the teaching of his predecessor, Pope Leo XIII, Pius XII was clearly urging Catholic scholars to embrace new discoveries that would assist them in understanding sacred scripture. Where *Providentissimus Deus* encouraged Catholic scholars to seek the "true meaning of the text," without explaining very clearly what that meant, *Divino Afflante Spiritu* would carefully describe what was meant by the "true meaning of the text" and explain how that meaning was to be found. "In the performance of this task let the interpreters bear in mind that their foremost and greatest endeavor should be to discern and define clearly that sense of the biblical words which is called *literal*. . . . Let them therefore by means of their knowledge of languages search out with all diligence the literal meaning of the words; . . . so that the mind of the author may be made abundantly clear" (*DAS*, 23; emphasis mine).

When Pius XII used the term "literal," he did not mean it the way we use it today to describe biblical fundamentalism. By "literal" he meant what the *biblical author* intended to convey and how the author's original reader understood what the biblical author wrote. All the scholarly tools and skills that had been developed since the late nineteenth century were to be learned by Catholic scholars or *exegetes* ("textual interpreters") and applied to the task of determining the literal meaning of the text.

Why is all this important? It is important because if I do not tightly bind my interpretation of the text to what the author genuinely intended, then I'm free to interpret the text in any way I like. Then I'll be like Humpty Dumpty in *Through the Looking Glass,* talking to Alice; I can say a word "means just what I choose it to mean."

While this example may be an oversimplification, it seems obvious that *Divino Afflante Spiritu* was telling Catholic scholars that they must catch up not only with the latest tools available to scholars but also with the scholarship of other Christian denominations. Catholic scholars had felt held back by the cautions of *Pascendi Dominici Gregis* and *Providentissimus Deus*. The cloud of Modernism had slowed Catholic progress in biblical studies. *Divino Afflante Spiritu* not only cleared the cloud and took the brakes off but also provided a papal urge to "get going!" That is why this papal encyclical is referred to as the *Magna Carta* of Catholic biblical scholarship. Catholic scholarship had been freed from the perceived constraints and fear of accusations of Modernism.

What Are the Tools for Scripture Scholarship?

The array of tools a biblical scholar uses for studying the Bible is immense. This chapter explains more about the discoveries, advances in biblical studies, and scholarly skills addressed by Pope Pius XII and generally collected in the large tool bag known as the "historical-critical method." This term includes many kinds of skills ranging from understanding the idioms of ancient writers to the grammatical study of ancient biblical texts.

Introduction to the Historical-Critical Method

At the outset, it needs to be clear that the word *critical* in historical-critical method has nothing to do with criticizing or being dismissive of scholars, Church authority, or religion. Critical in this case means "careful" or "data-driven" thinking. This means that the various scholarly skills that are included in the historical-critical method demand and are intent on reaching conclusions carefully, honestly, and objectively. *The Interpretation of the Bible in the Church*, a 1993 document of the Pontifical Biblical Commission, signed by Pope St. John Paul II and Cardinal

Joseph Ratzinger (Pope Benedict XVI), directly addressed the necessary role of the historical-critical method:

> The historical-critical method is the *indispensable* method for the scientific study of the meaning of ancient texts. Holy Scripture, inasmuch as it is the "Word of God in human language," has been composed by human authors in all its various parts and in all the sources that lie behind them. Because of this, its proper understanding not only admits the use of this method but actually requires it.[1]

It is the aim of historical-critical methods to arrive at the correct, justifiable interpretations of biblical texts whenever possible. This can be done in many ways. For example, a biblical scholar could analyze how stories about Jesus were told and retold orally before they were ever written down. Or, a scholar might do a side-by-side comparison of the ancient manuscripts of particular books of the Old or New Testament to determine which version is authentic. Another critical method might entail analyzing the various genres of writing found in the Bible. You likely already know that there are such genres as genealogies, poetry, accounts of miracles, stories of confrontation with opponents, ancient letter writing, parables, and many more.

One method of critical analysis studies the elements and structures of ancient Greek rhetoric so that such elements and structures can be identified within biblical texts. Think here especially of letters in the New Testament. You may be surprised to learn that twenty-one of the twenty-seven New Testament books are written in letter form, and these letters are replete with ancient rhetorical devices.

The list of such critical methods is actually quite long. What all of these critical methods have in common is that each seeks to understand the idioms, or the ways language is used, by those who shared biblical stories orally and by those who wrote them down. The Second Vatican Council document *Dei Verbum* put it this way:

> The fact is that truth is differently presented and expressed in the various types of historical writing, in prophetical and poetical texts, and in other forms of literary expression. Hence the exegete must look for that meaning which the sacred writers, in given situations and granted the circumstances of their time and culture, *intended to express* and did in fact express, through the medium of a contemporary literary form. . . . Attention must be paid both to the customary and characteristic patterns of perception, speech and narrative which prevailed in their time. (*DV*, 12, emphasis mine)

Once that intended meaning of the author can be established, then the text can be interpreted accurately. Now this does not mean that all scholars agree with the conclusions reached after the application of these methods—not by a long shot! But if the Catholic scholar is to arrive at the "literal" meaning of a text, these methods *must* be applied. All such approaches serve the same end: *to arrive at an accurate understanding of what the author wrote.*

Unpacking Culture and Idioms

Another tool for interpreting a biblical text involves understanding the particular cultures within the text and the culture surrounding period and place when and where the text was created. Consider just the single, fundamental cultural element of language. Now think about the thousands of idioms we use in English. These ways of speaking are usually pithy phrases that are colorful, but actually precisely convey very particular meanings. But meanings are far from the *literal* meaning of each of the individual words in the idiom. For example, my mother loved listening to Frank Sinatra songs. As a youth, I was not a fan. And I asked her why she thought he was so great. She told me, "I was a bobby-soxer and Frank Sinatra was the bee's knees."

I had no idea what she was saying. What is a bobby-soxer? What in the heck does "bee's knees" mean? Of course, later I learned that bobby-soxers were young girls in the late 1930s and early 1940s who traditionally wore ankle-length white socks and swooned over Frank Sinatra in much the same way a later generation of teenage girls would swoon over the Beatles. And "bee's knees" meant "really good" or "really sweet"—apparently derived from the fact that the knees of the insect bee is where all the sweet, good stuff is collected. But not many people who were not raised in her era would ever understand what my mom meant if they tried to dissect these phrases literally, word for word. What my mom was telling me was that when she was a young girl, she really liked Frank Sinatra.

If you and I would have trouble understanding what my mom meant by her answer about Frank Sinatra when we speak the same English language, imagine the thousands of such idioms used in ancient, non-English languages and the tremendous challenge of trying to accurately translate them into modern English. Additionally, in the case of the Old Testament, the texts of those biblical books are from an era that spans centuries. So the challenge is not just understanding Hebrew—the language of the Old Testament—but understanding the Hebrew used in the eighth century BC as well as the Hebrew used in the third century BC. By comparison, think of the English used by Shakespeare in sixteenth-century England and the English spoken and written today in the United States. Even within the same language, our vocabulary and our idioms have changed significantly over time. What a word or phrase meant four hundred years ago may not be what it means today. Idioms once popular and universally understood in one age may mean nothing to the readers from another age.

In chapter 5, we'll deal with some biblical idioms and biblical vocabulary that show just how important and challenging such elements can be in understanding what the biblical author was trying to say.

Discovering Variances in Writing Styles and the Importance of Rhetoric

Anyone who has read really old letters—the letters of Benjamin Franklin or Thomas Jefferson, for example—will instantly see how different today's *style* of writing is from the letter-writing style of the distant past. Not only is the vocabulary different, but the whole structure of old letters is different from our own. The tone of old letters generally seems very formal to us and the vocabulary often flowery and overly wordy.

Now go back even further in time to the ancient wrings of the Bible. First, of course, the language is different. Most of the Bible was written in either Hebrew or Greek. But there is more. Though the format of what is contained in the Bible is familiar to us—stories, histories, speeches, letters, etc.—the style seems very different to us, even foreign.

One reason for the difference in writing style has to do with the typical education and training of a biblical author. It, too, was very different from our own. Let's take the education of typical New Testament authors. As these were Greco-Roman times, the general model for education paralleled the education undertaken by an ancient lawyer. The classically educated man in that period was trained in the skill of rhetoric, or the art of persuasion. He learned how to convince a person, a crowd, an opponent, or a magistrate of his point of view. Imagine this training being like that of a modern debate class or a debate team. While law school students today primarily study the law, in the Greco-Roman world of New Testament times, they were trained to win an argument or the opinion of a crowd.

To learn how to sway opinions, a Greco-Roman student first studied grammar so that he could speak and write correctly. Then he would move on to study forms of writing and speaking. An important aspect of rhetoric was learning how to structure a speech or a written text to make an argument more effective and how to build up to a convincing conclusion. Within the overall structure of a written or spoken text, there were a plethora of other specific techniques or devices described in the rhetoric textbooks. (Aristotle wrote the classic text *Rhetoric* in the fourth century BC.)

Why is all of this important to those who study the Bible? Understanding this training of the ancient educated person allows exegetes today to discover several of the rhetorical devices contained within biblical texts. Experts have found samples of this kind of writing throughout the New Testament books.

For example, one rhetorical device of ancient writing is called *paraenesis*. This rhetorical style is designed to impart traditional moral teaching. We find this type of writing in several New Testament letters. *Diatribe* is another tool of ancient rhetoric. This device presents a forceful argument against one's opponent that often includes over-the-top exaggerations of the opponent's position or *ad hominem* personal attacks against the opponent. The listing of virtues and vices is another rhetorical device found in the Bible. There are many others. Each of these elements of rhetorical style is its own kind of sub-genre and therefore demands its own particular means of interpretation.

Understanding the style or genre of writing that you are reading is extremely important for interpreting the text and is an important step in getting us to what the Church demands: to determine the literal meaning of the text; that is, what the ancient author intended to say and how his first audience understood what he was saying. Knowing more about how the ancient writers wrote, and how their audiences listened and understood, keeps us from making erroneous interpretations and, most importantly, from reading into the text meanings the author did not intend.

Uncovering Details about the Lives of the Author and Audience

Another big help for interpreting biblical texts is learning more about the lives of the biblical author and the intended audience. Exegetes refer to this as the *Sitz im Leben*, German for "situation in life," and it refers to unpacking as many specific details as possible about the lives of both the biblical writer and the intended audience.

Let's take a modern example to see how unpacking one's life situation occurs. Imagine you are an attendant in a friend's wedding. After the wedding, you write a thank-you letter to the bride. In part of your note, you write:

> The reception was amazing! Who knew your uncle could do the Hokey Pokey so well! And the cake! I've never seen such a beautiful one. I was sure that you were going to try to smear that first piece in your husband's face but was so glad that you didn't. Then that tossing of the bouquet just before you both left! Who would have ever thought that your grandma would catch it! Ha! Imagine hers being the next wedding! I bet that made your grandpa a little nervous! Thanks again for letting me be a part of it all.

If you don't know that the "situation in life" being described in this letter is a recent wedding reception and you are not familiar with the customs of a modern American wedding, you might have difficulty understanding several parts of this note. Why is the uncle "doing the Hokey Pokey"? Who does such a dance anymore if they're not a child? And why would someone even think of smearing someone's face with a piece of cake? That's so weird. In the context of a wedding reception, however, none of what is described is unusual. It is only knowing the particular *Sitz im Leben* of the writer—wedding reception—that provides that needed hermeneutical key to open up the correct interpretation of the text.

Interestingly, *Sitz im Leben* works in two ways. Knowing the situation in the life of the writer and of the audience helps you to understand the meaning of the text. But, understanding the text also gives you a glimpse of who the author and his audience are and their *Sitz im Leben*. I'd bet that if you did not know that the above text was from a letter to a recently married person, you could have accurately inferred that "situation in life" just from what is mentioned in the text of the letter. Right?

For more than the last hundred years, the Church has demanded that Catholic interpreters use all these tools—all the skills of the historical-critical method—to arrive at the truth of the biblical text.

❮ 5 ❯

How Is Biblical Truth Conveyed?

The question of truth in scripture is a central one that must be explored in any introduction to biblical studies. The Second Vatican Council document *Dei Verbum* (as quoted in paragraph 107 of the *Catechism*) clearly states that the books of the Bible "firmly, faithfully, and without error teach that truth which God, for the sake of our salvation, wished to see confided to the Sacred Scriptures" (*DV*, 11). This means that truth and inerrancy ("without error") are synonymous in speaking of the Bible.

To further answer the question "Is the Bible true?" you have to first ask yourself whether you mean that everything in the Bible is literally, scientifically, or historically true. If that is your question, the answer is no. Not everything in the Bible is science or history, though some of both are in the Bible. Rather, as pointed out previously, the Bible is made up of different literary forms. These include poetry, allegories, fables, speeches, census lists, and many other types of literature. Is the Bible religiously true? The answer is an unequivocal yes. But to determine the religious truth, we have to look more thoroughly at the genre of the biblical writings.

So let's recast the question and not ask "Is the Bible true?" but "How is biblical truth conveyed?"

Examining Genres

Let's start by taking a look at a couple of examples that are not in the Bible. Consider, first, the classic Shakespearean tragedy *Romeo and Juliet*. We all know this is not literally a "true" story. There was no such young couple in Verona. There were no families named Capulet and Montague. No such family rivalries resulted in tragic deaths. It is not a true story!

And yet this famous drama very clearly *conveys* truth. Young lovers often run afoul of their respective families. Family feuds hurt the innocent and often result in terrible tragedies. In these ways, and more, the story of Romeo and Juliet does convey truth, but it does so by means of a particular genre of dramatic art called "tragedy."

One more example from outside the Bible: You may be familiar with a segment on the television program *Saturday Night Live* called "Weekend Update." To refresh your memory, this is a satirical parody of the evening news where two comedians take the role of news anchors. Now, imagine you have a neighbor who is a recent immigrant from a farming village in an Eastern European country. Let's call her Mrs. Marvich. She has only been in this country for a few months, and while she's learned English pretty well, she is not yet versed in all of the nuances of American culture. Mrs. Marvich has watched the regular evening news in her own country and is familiar with the format of most evening news programs. And then she stumbles upon the "Weekend Update" late one Saturday night after moving to America. Can you imagine Mrs. Marvich being confused by what she is seeing and hearing, especially if she tried to interpret it as the real news? What she is watching is not the news! She's watching a particular genre of comedy called *satire*.

Now, let's transfer these lessons to looking at some examples from the book of Psalms. Read the following texts:

> The earth rocked and shook; the foundations of the
> mountains trembled; they shook as his wrath flared

> up. Smoke rose from his nostrils, a devouring fire from his mouth; it kindled coals into flame. (Ps 18:8–9)

> [God] makes Lebanon leap like a calf, and Sirion like a young bull. (Ps 29:6)

> Let the rivers clap their hands, the mountains shout with them for joy. (Ps 98:8)

Of course, the earth never quaked as a result of God's anger, nor did smoke or fire or flaming coals ever emerge from his mouth. Likewise, God did not make Sirion (Mount Lebanon) jump like a young bull. Mountains did not shout, and rivers have no hands to clap. Undoubtedly, you realize that these passages from the Psalms are *poetic*. While these things did not literally happen, the authors imaginatively used these poetic images to convey truthful messages.

Let's take another example, from a famous text in Luke 10:29–37. Jesus says here: "A man fell victim to robbers as he went down from Jerusalem to Jericho. They stripped and beat him and went off leaving him half dead." You probably recognize these words as the introduction to the famous parable of the Good Samaritan. But we know that there was no "man" who "went down from Jerusalem to Jericho." And there was no Samaritan who stopped and helped the poor man.

One could, *strictly speaking*, say that Jesus is not telling the truth here. It's a story that Jesus made up. But we all understand that Jesus is using this genre called *parable* and it is the nature of a parable to make up a story using ordinary people and events in order to make a strong point. Yes, strictly speaking, this is not a factual story. It is not true. But the story *conveys* truth.

Let's take one more example: the entire book of Revelation, the last book of the Bible. This is a particularly important example because the book of Revelation conveys many terrible "visions" of divine intervention in our world. You likely have heard some of these visions being interpreted to spread dread and foreboding concerning Christ's second coming. Some Christian groups and individual Christians have interpreted these visions to offer very concrete and specific predictions about the future of the world. (Think about the *Left Behind* series and accompanying interpretations of this enigmatic biblical book.)

The book of Revelation uses a highly symbolic form of writing, a genre known as *apocalypse*. Apocalyptic writing emerged in late Old Testament times. Part of the book of Daniel is written in this genre. Revelation used this weirdly imaginative style of the apocalyptic genre with elements like visions of exotic beasts, scenes of great conflict, the use of numbers, and much more to convey its message. Interpreting the truth of the book of Revelation *literally* is just not possible. This genre, for example, demands a strict dualism. In apocalyptic literature there is only good and bad; it allows no moral shades of grey. The element of truth of apocalyptic writing from the book of Revelation is easier to decipher once we understand the genre of literature with which it is written—and the requirements of that particular genre.

Knowing the genre of the literature you are reading, a television show you are watching, or the genre of any other means of communication informs how you interpret it. This seems obvious and really simple. However, we have to remember two things: genres of literature and art vary from culture to culture and, more importantly, genres change throughout history. Genres immediately recognizable to a reader or audience in antiquity are not so readily recognized by us today.

How Does a Scripture Scholar Uncover Biblical Truth?

Some of the examples shared in the previous section should make you aware that biblical truth is not always readily apparent. So how, then, can it be uncovered? The 1964 Pontifical Biblical

Commission document *Sancta Mater Ecclesia* (*SME*) (*Instruction on the Historical Truth of the Gospels*), focusing on interpretation of the gospels but applying to the totality of scripture study, said that "the exegete will not fulfill his task—finding out what the sacred writers said and really intended [literal meaning]—unless he considers all the factors involved in the origin and composition of the Gospels, and makes proper use of the sound findings of recent investigations" (*SME*, 10). Those who study scripture are strongly urged to use the historical-critical methods "to shed clearer light on the meaning intended by God through the sacred writer" (*SME*, 12).

The commission's later document, *Interpretation of the Bible in the Church* (*IBC*), repeated the demand that the exegete is responsible to determine the "literal sense" of the biblical text; that is, what the original inspired author intended to communicate. Those who study a biblical text must, to the extent possible, anchor their interpretation in the intention of the biblical writer. If this is not done, as I suggested before, the text can mean just about whatever the reader wants it to mean.

Both documents make it clear that all resources, intelligence, and skills available to the exegete are to be used to determine the literal meaning of the biblical writer. This can be difficult considering some of the cultural, historical, and language barriers described previously.

Consider: How do we translate the Greek text of the gospels, written in the late first century AD? What did the idioms of first century Greek mean? What genres of communication were known by and typical of the first followers of Jesus? What was the *Sitz im Leben* of the authors and their audiences? And, to complicate things further, let's remember that Jesus and his followers were primarily Aramaic speakers. Yet the written text of the gospels is in Greek. That means that Jesus' original spoken words—his stories, parables, and homilies—and all the oral traditions of his first followers were originally in Aramaic. Needless to say, ancient Aramaic, like all languages, had its own peculiar idioms and genres.

The Revelation of Scripture Is Truly without Error

Much like the patron of my religious community, St. Francis of Assisi, St. John Chrysostom, an early Church Father, was consumed by contemplation of the love of God. Both St. Francis and St. John understood that the heart of the Christian faith is the conviction that "God so loved the world" (Jn 3:16) that he would seek to share every aspect of the lives of his beloved—human beings—by becoming one of us. St. John Chrysostom was a great preacher (*chrysostom* means "golden-mouthed") and one of the greatest theologians of the early Church. He understood that the key to understanding sacred scripture was in meditating on the incarnational love of God for the world.

St. John Chrysostom also understood that because God so loved us, he accommodated his communication to his people to *our* way of speaking and understanding so "that we may come to know his ineffable and loving kindness" (*DV*, 13). In other words, God's love for us compelled him to speak to us in ways that we could understand. God spoke to us through the inspired authors of scripture in the jargon of his people.

Think about how this is so. When God spoke to his chosen people through the prophets through the several centuries of their Old Testament struggles, it was in language and with a message that these one-time wandering former slaves could understand. When Jesus addressed his followers, he spoke to them in their Aramaic language using stories and parables that they could understand. And, then, when the inspired New Testament writers recorded the words of Jesus and his first followers, they translated the original words of Jesus and his first followers into Greek, the common language of the Gentile converts, so that *they* could understand.

The Church does the same thing. She prays and studies the sacred scriptures so that she can interpret them accurately and translate them carefully into the ever-changing languages that accommodate the styles, genres, idioms, poetry, and more of the many languages of people throughout the world so that they can understand.

On November 18, 1965, Pope Paul VI promulgated the most authoritative teaching of the Church regarding sacred scripture—the dogmatic constitution produced by the Second Vatican Council, *Dei Verbum* (*On Divine Revelation*). The first chapter speaks of the role of language—that is, words—in God's Revelation:

> This plan of revelation is realized by deeds and words having an inner unity: the deeds wrought by God in the history of salvation manifest and confirm the teaching and realities signified by the words, while the words proclaim the deeds and clarify the mystery contained in them. By this revelation then, the deepest truth about God and the salvation of man shines out for our sake in Christ, who is both the mediator and the fullness of all revelation. (*DV*, 2)

This final phrase—the "salvation of man"—becomes the means by which the Church can logically answer the question of truth in the Bible.

That is, the Bible is concerned with the salvation of humans. Biblical "errors" concerning such things as science, biology, and history are inconsequential and do not threaten the truth and inerrancy of God's Revelation in the Bible. The aim of God's inspiration of the biblical authors is that they communicate exactly what God wished to communicate—that which is true—for the sake of our salvation. The Bible is not without error concerning the movement of heavenly bodies. There are mistakes of history and biographical details within the Bible.

But the scriptures convey truth to us concerning those things necessary for our salvation. I had a scripture professor in college who frequently reminded us: "The Bible is not written to tell us how the heavens go. It is written to tell us how to go to heaven." In this objective and toward this end—our salvation—the Bible is without error and does convey unalterable truth.

◄ 6 ►

Why Is Geography Important in Biblical Studies?

The first and most fundamental context for understanding the Bible is its geography. But, *why* is understanding the geography of the region where the Bible was created so important? The three deceptively simple answers are: Egypt, Egypt, and Egypt. While Egypt does not figure much explicitly in the biblical narrative after the great Exodus of Hebrew slaves, this large land, this swath of mostly desert, is almost always lurking in the background of most of the books of the Bible, silently exercising its immense influence over the ancient geopolitical movements of the region. And those geopolitical movements profoundly influenced much of the creation of both the Old Testament and New Testament.

The land of Egypt is a brown box of sand tied up in the middle with blue and green ribbons. The brown box of sand is the desert landmass that makes up most of Egypt. The blue ribbon that ties up the region is the 750-mile Nile River that runs through it. The green ribbons are the irrigated fertile strips of land running along both sides of the river. This river, unlike so many in the world, flows from south to north for the full length of the land of Egypt. Its source is the dense African highlands

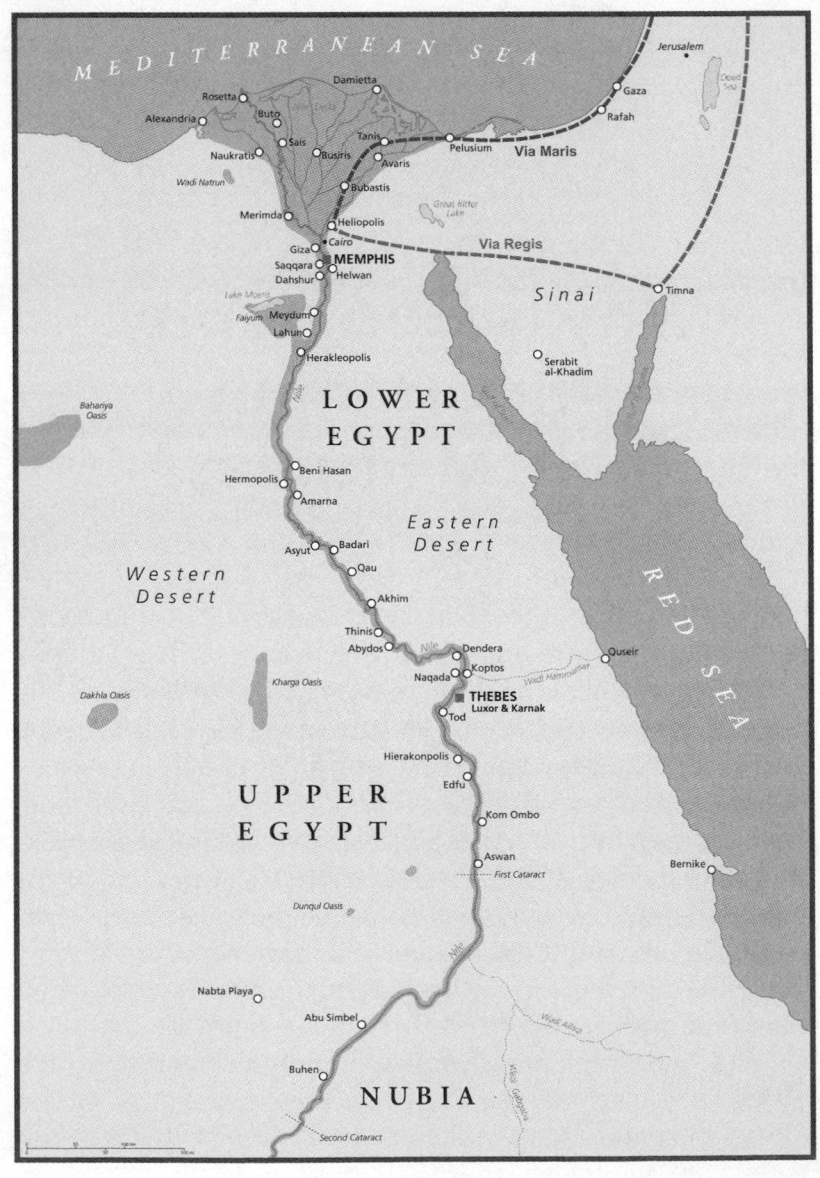

far to the south of Egypt with their heavy rainfall. From there the river flows downhill, to the north, without tributaries within Egypt, to the low-lying delta region of northern Egypt and out into the Mediterranean Sea.

While only about 3 percent of Egypt consists of the Nile valley and delta around the river, this valley is extraordinarily fertile. The Nile valley is also twice blest. As the rainfall from the southern highlands of Africa spills into the fertile valleys, way to the south of Egypt, and converges into the Nile River bed, alluvial soil, rich in nutrients, comes with it. Thus Egypt is the beneficiary not only of a dependable and predictable water source, but also of the fertile soil carried by the water. In effect, the water brings its own fertilizer with it. Nutrient-rich soil, fresh water, and almost constant sunshine all conspire to make the Nile River valley one of the richest agricultural strips of land in the world. In antiquity, one acre of irrigated Egyptian soil could produce three times the amount of grain as an acre of any other land bordering the Mediterranean.

The Nile River also serves Egypt as a transportation and communication system, even today, as it was in biblical times. The ancient historian Herodotus was correct when he referred to Egypt as the "gift of the Nile." All these reasons combined to make the land of Egypt extremely wealthy and therefore much sought after by other nations through the centuries in which the biblical events took place and the Bible was formed.

The Location of Egypt Contributed to Its Stability

The geography of Egypt is also somewhat unique in how it contributed to the stability of ancient Egypt, a stability that lasted for nearly three thousand years. The Mediterranean Sea forms the northern border of the country. In the east, Egypt is bordered by a rugged terrain of hills and mountains, stretching east and south into the inhospitable Sinai Desert. In the west is the Libyan Desert, a portion of the larger Sahara Desert. This part of the Sahara is desolate and waterless. At the southern border of ancient Egypt was Nubia, a nation dominated for centuries by the ancient Egyptians. Pharaohs would often go to Nubia to plunder slaves, herds, ostriches, or anything else his majesty wanted from their southern neighbor. Through most of its history, Egypt feared nothing from the south and was protected to the east and west by inhospitable terrain.

All in all, ancient Egypt was in the enviable position, militarily speaking, of being surrounded by natural defenses against foreign invasion. To the north is the sea, from which it only occasionally suffered incursions from the Sea People, the ancestors of the Philistines. In the east, the almost impassible terrain of the Sinai and its mountains kept unwanted military threats at bay. Here the one exception or entrance through this lunar-like Sinai terrain was in the far north, along the southeastern shore of the Mediterranean Sea where the Egyptians built an ancient highway called "The Way of Horus." This narrow roadway, pressed against the coastal plain, passed north through the land of Israel.

Egypt's northeastern border with Israel had this narrow, traversable strip, up against the sea coast, through which armies could pass. But since any outside aggressors would be severely bottlenecked if they attempted passage though this strip, Egypt could, and often did, easily repel such attacks from this direction. In fact, though ancient Egypt did not have colonies in foreign lands, the nation always sought and achieved military control of this roadway and coastal area in Israel and even further north into Syria as well. What geography did not provide by way of natural protection from the south and east, Egypt provided by its military force. In short, Egypt was "sitting pretty" on the surface of the globe. It had the natural resources and natural fortifications on almost every flank to protect those resources. This is why for three thousand years we can speak of ancient Egypt's culture as rich and as constant, almost as monolithic as its famous obelisks. While certainly there were occasional incursions of foreign armies and even intermittent foreign domination, rarely was Egypt's culture disrupted for long. Egypt had the means to keep its tremendous agricultural wealth secure.

It was these rich resources, this agricultural output, that tempted all would-be world dominators from the ninth century BC all the way to the time of the foundation of the Roman Empire in the first century BC to conquer and control Egypt.

The Geography of Israel

Israel is a section, a narrow section, of the Fertile Crescent. The Fertile Crescent is the great green arc that comes over from the north and east. In the east it begins with the fertile green of the Tigris and Euphrates River systems (ancient Mesopotamia and present-day Iraq), heads northwest and then turns south and runs in and through Israel's fertile Jordan River bed. The green crescent is briefly interrupted along the sea coast by a small patch of the Sinai Desert and then crosses the northern Sinai Peninsula and reconnects to the western end of the fertile cresecent, the green Nile valley of Egypt. This makes it a narrow green piece that just barely connects the fertile green of the Jordan River valley to the Nile water system.

It is Israel's geography that makes it the connecting piece of the crescent between Mesopotamia in the east and Egypt in the west. The mountainous highlands of the northern part of the crescent, with its water systems, begin a downward drainage into the depression in northern Israel that collects much of the water into the Sea of Galilee and then heads south as the Jordan River exits the Sea of Galilee. The rains and this body of water fertilize this northern part of Israel and are the source for the agricultural productivity of the area. The river leaves the basin of the Sea of Galilee and makes its way south in a trough—a very deep trough—down through Israel, finally dumping into the Dead Sea. I say "dumping" advisedly since the Dead Sea is landlocked and has no exit. The water that flows into it stays there, much of it evaporating in the scorching desert sun.

The Jordan River follows this course because the topography of Israel here is marked by a geological phenomenon known as the Jordan Rift, a deep gorge running almost the full length of Israel, which cuts more deeply into the earth's crust here than in any other place on the planet. Standing at its deepest point, near Jericho, one is standing the farthest below sea level a person can get and still be on dry land. The river runs through this deep cut in the earth's crust, draining the highlands and mountains of Israel as it flows south to the Dead Sea. This gorge also provided a natural route for another important roadway called the "King's Highway" or the "Via Regis."

Unlike Egypt, Israel also gets water from rain. Rainwater contributes to the Jordan River's volume, but the quick runoff of rainwater leaves the more fertile north and heads downhill, south into the Dead Sea. Yet in the south, some of this rain-water drains into *wadis* through the mineral-rich sands of the Judean desert. There the runoff takes on more and more mineral salts from the desert floor until the water can no longer support marine life and becomes impossible to drink. This is how the Dead Sea "got" dead! Not much lives in or near the Dead Sea. This runoff water is so rich in mineral salts—more than five times saltier than sea water—that on the shores of the Dead Sea, one can see great salt formations developing an eerie white crust along the water's edge. Its shores are covered with these salt crystals. Unable to flow out of the basin of the Dead Sea, the evaporating water leaves its minerals behind to poison the water. It is this high mineral content that gives the water of the Dead Sea its famous buoyancy. To say that one can swim "in" the Dead Sea is somewhat misleading. In fact, one swims more "on" the sea than in it.

Near here, to the west, the northern border of the Sinai Desert, is the thinnest portion of the Fertile Crescent. The section of the arc, up against the Mediterranean Sea, connecting Egypt with

Israel, is the least green of any portion of the Fertile Crescent. Water is scarce along this part. Ancient peoples traveling along the Way of Horus from Israel to Egypt had to bring water with them, and they had to know well the location of the occasional oases which sparsely dot the terrain of the northern Sinai Peninsula. It was these two parallel highways, the Way of Horus (later called Via Maris) and the Via Regis that traversed the length of Israel, connecting Israel to Egypt in the west and to the peoples of Mesopotamia and Persia in the east. Think of these two roads passing through Israel as the narrowest point in the middle of a great global hourglass. At one end was the rich land of Egypt and at the other end were the lands of Mesopotamia—Assyria, Babylonia, and Persia—all connected "in the middle" and by these two narrow highways.

These roads, and the peoples of various cultures who traveled them, had a great influence on the Jews, and later the first Christians, living in Israel.

Egypt Influenced Much of Biblical History

Scripture scholar Fr. Felix Just, S.J., devised (with a little help from yours truly) a rather clever two-sentence mnemonic device to recall the list of countries that at one point in history held dominance over Israel.

Eat At Bill's! Philly's Greatest Restaurant!

This silly phrase translates for our purposes this way: "Eat" is Egypt. "At" is Assyria. "Bill's" is Babylon. "Philly's" is Persia. "Greatest" is Greece (of the famous Alexander the Great). "Restaurant" is Rome. These are the "major players" in chronological order that caused the great crises of Israel's history. It's important to remember that the books of the Bible were written within the contexts of these geopolitical movements—most of them tragic for Israel—that passed through the narrow strip of land on those two highways.

The role of Egypt in the early historical books of the Old Testament is pretty clear. Think of the famines that first drove Abraham's family to migrate to Egypt and the troubles they encountered there with Pharaoh. Think of the later famine that required the sons of Jacob to travel to Egypt for food after their hatred for their brother Joseph caused him to be left in the desert and taken to Egypt as a slave. It was Egypt's agricultural wealth and Joseph's rise to power in Egypt that drove the whole of the patriarchal families of Jacob en masse to migrate to Egypt at the time of that second famine. The subsequent enslavement of their descendants would launch the central event of Jewish history, the Exodus.

It was the Exodus of these slaves escaping Egypt that was the context for giving the Torah to Moses on Mount Sinai. Arriving at the Promised Land, essentially returning where their ancestors had lived centuries before under Abraham, Isaac, and Jacob, precipitated the long biblical accounts of "the settlement period." These accounts include the stories of Joshua, the rise of the judges, and Israel's struggles with their hostile neighbors. These struggles would spark the rise of the monarchy beginning with Saul, David, and Solomon, and the long histories of the kings of Israel and the later separated kingdom of Judah. All of these events are told in the Old Testament and are directly connected to Egypt and the geography of the region.

Prophetic books would have as their background the great crises sparked by the domination of Assyria ("At"), Babylon ("Bill's"), and Persia ("Philly's"), whose conquering forces all followed the two ancient roads through Israel to Egypt. Assyria went through Israel to take power from Egypt in the eighth century BC. Amos, the first writing prophet of Israel, wrote just prior to Assyrian intervention. In the sixth century BC, Babylon rose and began moving east, heading for Egypt and conquering a weakened Assyria. The major prophets—Isaiah, Jeremiah, and

Ezekiel—all shared messages of hope during this period with the Jews who were suffering through the calamites of these world powers trying to conquer and hold on to the wealth of Egypt.

In the next phase of history, Persia's rising power emboldened them to head west to Egypt. Persia would conquer and dominate Egypt from 550 to 330 BC. On their way to Egypt, the Persians would occupy ancient Turkey. This made it quite easy later for Persia to advance into Europe. At that point, Persia also began to threaten the Greeks ("Greatest").

The Greeks, feeling the pressure from the Persians just across the Bosporus, finally were forced by a Macedonian king, Philip II, to unite the armies of their independent city-states to confront the Persian threat. With this large combined force of the Greek city-states, Philip was able to push the Persians back from the edge of Europe all the way into Turkey. There, Philip was assassinated around 336 BC. He was succeeded by his young, twenty-three-year-old son, Alexander.

Alexander the Great succeeded far beyond any imagining in driving the Persians out of Turkey and Egypt, through old Assyria and ancient Babylon. Alexander continued his conquest even beyond Persia. He conquered every place his soldiers marched, ultimately all the way into the subcontinent of India, to the Indus River. Greek domination of the Fertile Crescent would last for over two centuries. For Alexander, too, it was the wealth of Egypt that drew him, even as he pursued the forces of Persia.

Alexander the Great was not just a warrior of the battlefield; he was a "culture warrior" as well. He populated much of the conquered territories with his soldiers. These soldiers took local wives and built Greek cities throughout these vast conquered territories and thus implanted Greek culture all over the map. Even the Greek language, a simplified version called Koine Greek, would become the *lingua franca* ("common language") of all these regions. This form of Greek culture is known as Hellenistic culture, to distinguish it from the culture of "classical" Greek of the earlier centuries.

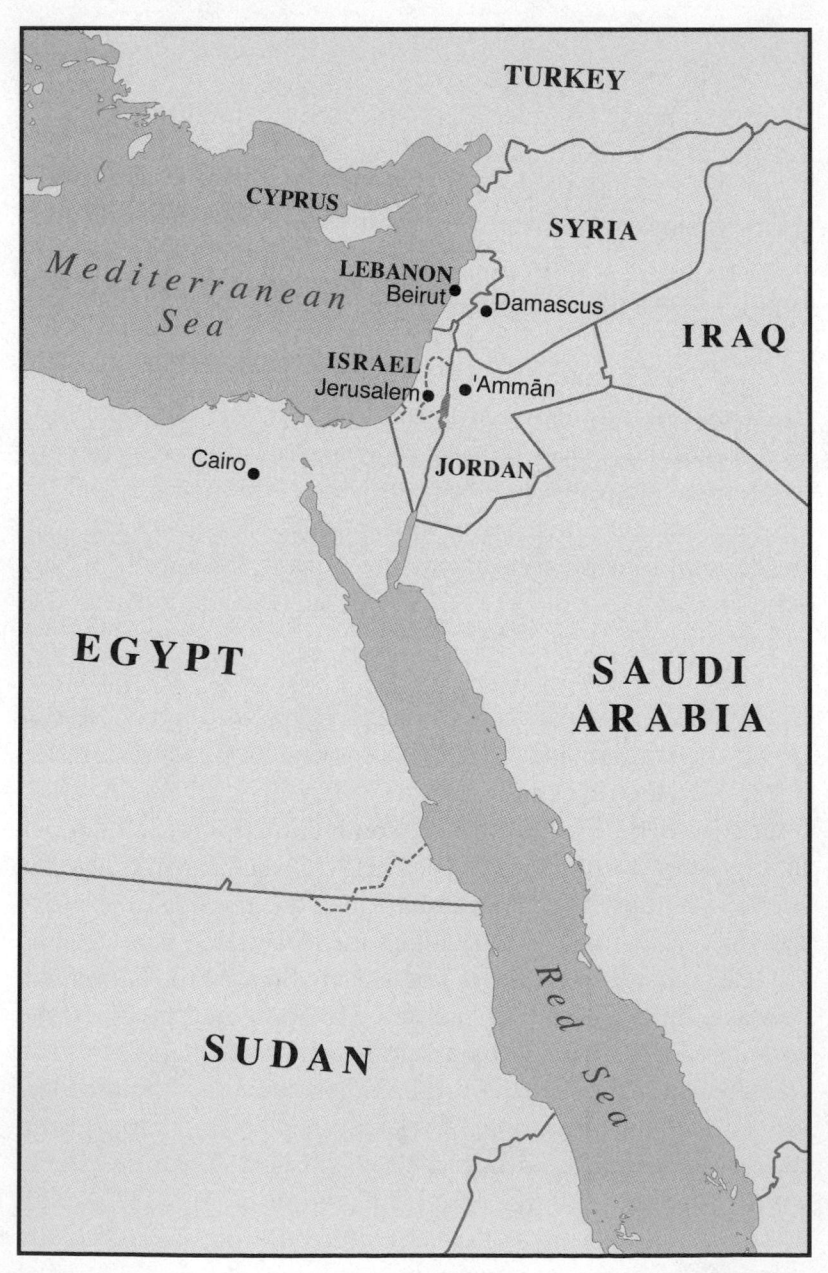

This Hellenistic culture would take hold throughout Mesopotamia, but would also be adopted in Egypt and farther west by the rising city-state on the west coast of Italy, in the region known as Latium, Rome ("Rome"). This city, struggling to expand its control of the Mediterranean Sea, would defeat her great commercial and maritime rival, the city-state of Carthage in North Africa, first in the battle of Zama, in 202 BC. In another definitive battle in 146 BC, Rome would utterly destroy Carthage and begin her rise as a great maritime and military power.

The Roman Empire and its Hellenized culture form the backdrop for all of the New Testament. Jesus is born at the end of the reign of Herod the Great, a Jewish monarch installed by the Roman Senate. Jesus' life and ministry occurred under the rule of Roman governorship, Roman taxation, and the reigns of puppet monarchs, descendants of Herod the Great, who were supported by Roman emperors. Evidence for these occurrences comes from the gospels. The early Church's formation under Roman rule is described in the Acts of the Apostles and in some of the New Testament letters. The apocalyptic visions of the book of Revelation are projected upon the backdrop of the Roman imperial persecutions of Christians.

Each of the dominators of Israel from the Egyptians to the Romans ("Eat at Bill's! Philly's Greatest Restaurant!")—regardless of various military interests—were drawn in some way by the agricultural richness of the land of Egypt. This means that each of these conquering nations passed to and from Egypt along those two highways through that bottleneck of land along the Mediterranean Sea that was Israel. Whether clashing, conquering, or retreating, their eyes were always on the richness of Egypt. Israel was never the real target or goal of these world conquerors. Simply put, Israel was merely, geographically speaking, in the way.

≺ 7 ≻

Where and When Was the Bible Created? (and Other Related Questions)

The two interrogatives that form the title of this chapter are often confused. Trying to answer the "where" part of the question means you first have to discover "when" the various books of the Bible were created. Or, you have to answer the two questions together.

As mentioned in chapter 6, the Torah, the first five books of the Bible, recorded God's communication around a historic event in Egypt: the escape of the Hebrew slaves. It is believed by many biblical scholars (although disputed as well) that the oldest piece of the Old Testament is the "Song of Miriam," also known as the "Song of the Sea." It is sung by Aaron's sister—"Sing to the Lord, for he is gloriously triumphant; horse and chariot he has cast into the sea" (Ex 15:21)—and is thought by some to have been sung spontaneously immediately after the Israelites crossed the Red Sea, hence the speculation that it was connected to that event and is the oldest biblical text. If this text dates back to very near the time of the Exodus itself, then it can be dated somewhere around 1250 BC. The place of origin would likewise be established as just outside Egypt near the Red Sea.

Dating the "youngest" text of the Old Testament, that is, the most recently created book of the Old Testament, is more complicated. It is not certain which of the Old Testament books is the "newest." Some additions to the book of Daniel are dated by experts to around 80 BC. Others believe the book of Wisdom, composed with a combination of Greek and Jewish style, may be more recent, around the mid-first century BC. If we say that the last bits of the Old Testament were written in approximately 100 BC and that the oldest parts were written near 1250 BC, then the timespan of the formation of all the books of the Old Testament is at least one thousand years.

The texts of the New Testament were mostly written in the eastern part of the Roman Empire, near the eastern end of the Mediterranean Sea. This means most of the New Testament was composed in Israel, Syria, present-day Turkey, and the islands of the eastern Mediterranean. It is possible that the Gospel of Mark was written in Rome. The oldest texts of the New Testament are the letters of St. Paul, with the oldest of these likely the First Letter to the Thessalonians, dated between AD 48 and 51. Most scholars, but not all, believe the Second Letter of Peter was the last book of the New Testament written, sometime around AD 120–125. If these opinions are both true, then the timespan for the formation of the New Testament is between AD 48 and 125, less than one century. So that's the timeframe, the "when" of biblical writing. The "where" is a bit more complicated because determining where the Bible was created must include cultural issues.

Understanding the Cultures Surrounding the Biblical Texts

A far more complex question than determining the timeframe and locations of origin of the biblical texts is: What *cultures* did the biblical books come from? This is an important consideration if a biblical student wishes to follow the guidance of the Church in determining the intent of the biblical authors and how their audiences understood what they wrote.

Again, a reminder: the regions of the Old Testament and New Testament world were under several successive ruling nations (Eat At Bill's! Philly's Greatest Restaurant!), each impressing aspects of its culture upon a dominated people. So not only did the geopolitical and military influences of these conquerors have profound effects on *what* was written in the biblical books, but the various cultures of the conquerors and occupiers also had profound effects on *how* the biblical writers wrote what they did. Among other things impacted by culture were the language, literary images, styles of writing, allusions, and references a biblical writer used.

Let's consider a contemporary American example to explain what I mean. My origins are in the Midwest. When I asked my good friend and classmate, Fr. Albért Haase, O.F.M., who is from New Orleans, what his plans were for lunch, his reply was, "I'm gonna have a po' boy for lunch today." Now if you are not from New Orleans and if you knew nothing about New Orleans foods, you might think, "Oh, Fr. Albért is hosting a young man for lunch today who has little or no money." But, if you *were* from New Orleans and knew something of New Orleans cuisine, you would immediately understand that Fr. Albért is having a sandwich that is like a sub (or in Philadelphia a hoagie) for lunch. Knowing this bit about his culture is the only way you could have correctly interpreted what he said. The exact same thing is true for understanding biblical texts.

You can understand the multiple challenges a translator has in translating the original Hebrew, Aramaic, and Greek biblical texts to languages of today. The translator must understand the culture or cultures from which the biblical writer emerged, and also know very well the culture of the target audience for which the text was intended. Both the culture of the writer and the culture of the audience are geographically and historically specific. A word used in one place and time may have a completely different meaning than the same word used in another place at a different time.

The Challenge of Translating Inspired Texts

The biblical texts being translated to modern languages are religiously privileged texts. This adds another layer of difficulty for the translator. Because these texts are the inspired and inerrant Word of God, the translator approaches them not only with technical skill but with reverence and respect. There are generations of Jewish and Christian translators before us who have taken care to maintain the original integrity of these texts. During the period before the invention of the printing press, maintaining this integrity meant carefully copying the biblical text by hand on parchment or papyrus. Similarly, the classic teachings *about* the biblical texts from Church Fathers and other Church authorities must be attended to by also being translated and copied carefully and correctly. Only in this effort can we have an accurate understanding of what past biblical experts believed about a text and what guided their interpretation.

Let me share an example of a challenge of translating the Bible. Many years ago scholars translated the Hebrew word *pas* that was used to describe the famous coat given to Joseph by his father Jacob in Genesis 37:3 to mean "many colored." Both the ancient Greek translation of the Old Testament—called the

Septuagint—and the Latin translation—called the Vulgate—incorrectly suggested the word *pas* meant "many colored" or "elaborately colored or decorated." Martin Luther took his cue from the Septuagint and also translated *pas* to mean "many colored" for Protestant Bibles. But, in fact, later scholarship correctly revealed that the Hebrew word *pas* means "long sleeved" or "a tunic that reaches to both the feet and wrists." This is an entirely different meaning and renders a new perspective on the title of the famous musical *Joseph and the Amazing Technicolor Dreamcoat*! Modern editions of the Bible often include a footnote at Genesis 37:3 stating something such as that the coat was "formerly rendered as a 'coat of many colors.'"

Now this particular example of an error in translation does not have serious theological or religious consequences, but for the faithful who have read and prayed over this beautiful story about the youthful Joseph, such a change can be disturbing. When such a person reads a newer translation of the Bible and finds a change (for example, to "long ornamented tunic" in the *New American Bible Revised Edition*), it sometimes raises questions having to do with the stability or even inerrancy of familiar biblical texts. They might ask: "How can God's eternal Word be changed?" Or, "Who did this?" And, "Why was this text changed from what I have always known?" It is the deeply held religious nature of the biblical texts that adds this extra layer of complexity and challenge to the task of the translator.

In part II, we will look more in depth at some words and phrases from the New Testament after critically studying their origin and meaning dependent on their language, culture, and translation.

≺ 8 ≻

How Were Ancient Bibles Produced?

Let's back up and address the question of how the words of the Bible even got onto the pages before you. The Bible texts have taken many circumnavigations to get to where they are now.

When the biblical authors decided to put the words in writing, they had no computers, typewriters, or printing presses. They wrote in Hebrew, Aramaic, or Greek on papyrus pages or on parchment (pages made from animal skins). These pages were then either pasted together, end to end into long strands, and rolled around wooden rods as scrolls or folded and sewn together into book form called a codex. When their original pages wore out and had to be replaced, someone had to hand copy the original to make new copies. This entire process was slow and complex. In the course of time, the scroll would go out of fashion altogether and the codex, the book form, would replace it.

Despite the fact that copies were being made by professional scribes and copiers, who were highly skilled in their accuracy and penmanship, errors still crept into their work. Also, the written form of Hebrew and Aramaic uses no vowels or punctuation. Imagine a text with no capital letters, no periods, and no indentations to mark new paragraphs. These irregularities for both Jewish and Christian scholars in later eras caused suspicion as to just *how* the original texts were to be read and understood. I'll share more on those issues later in the chapter. First, let's address details about the mechanics of copying a biblical manuscript and the material it was copied on.

More about Papyrus and Parchment

Between papyrus and parchment, papyrus was by far the cheaper material for recording texts. It was also the least durable. Parchment was very expensive but lasted for a much longer time.

Papyrus is made from the papyrus plant—called "bulrush" in old translations of the Bible (see Isaiah 19:7, for example). The papyrus plant has tall, three-sided reeds. When the outer skin of this reed is shaved, the underlying layer is very fibrous and durable and can be easily stripped off. After this layer is stripped off each of the three sides of the stalk, the strips are laid horizontally, on a flat surface, parallel to each other. Then a second layer is laid perpendicularly on top, across the first layer. These two layers are then pressed tightly together and dried. The gum and fluids in these strips act like glue, so the pressed layers hold together and, once dried, the surfaces can be rubbed and burnished into smooth writing surfaces.

Sheets of papyrus could then be glued together, end to end, to form long rolls for literary works to be written on. These long strips were then rolled up around two wooden rods, one at either end, into scrolls. The papyrus sheets could also be folded, collected together, and sewn into a binding to form the book or codex. The quality of the papyrus varied. One could print (using ink from ground-up minerals) clearly and smoothly on expensive papyrus. Cheaper pieces of papyrus could be glued together to form wrapping paper or used in making baskets and occasionally even used to line coffins.

The ancient Egyptians were especially skilled at making papyrus. They had an abundant supply of papyrus plants growing in the delta and along the Nile River, and they had centuries to perfect their skills. Given what we know of the weather of Egypt, it should not surprise us that most discoveries of ancient papyrus are made in Egypt. That's because the preservation of papyrus has two major challenges. Papyrus does not hold up well in conditions that are either too moist or too dry. Moisture causes the papyrus to soften and decay; with intense dryness, the papyrus becomes brittle and easily cracks into fragments. Conditions had to be those of Goldilocks ("just right") for ancient papyrus to survive antiquity. Egypt provided those conditions. Some documents written on papyrus have been discovered that date back to 2,500 BC!

Parchment is another matter entirely—literally, another matter. Parchment is made from animal skins of goats, sheep, or cows. The word "parchment" actually comes from the name of the ancient city of Pergamum. This city was located in western Turkey, near the modern city of Bergama, and was already a prominent city before the time of Alexander the Great. It later supported and submitted to Roman power in the second century BC. *And* it was famous for its production of parchment.

The Roman naturalist Pliny the Elder, writing in the first century AD, said that parchment was invented in Pergamum in order to compete economically with the city of Alexandria, in Egypt, which was dominating the world trade in papyrus. True or not, this city became literally synonymous with this form of writing material.

The term parchment is used generically for skins derived from goats, sheep, or cows and occasionally from ibexes and antelope. But the quality of the skins taken from these animals varied. The best quality of all parchment came from the skin of calves. This kind of parchment is distinguished by the name "vellum." You might notice that this word is derived from the same Latin word that gives us the word "veal." Both designate something which comes from a young cow. There is actually an even better-quality parchment that comes from the skin of *unborn* calves. This very exclusive and very expensive parchment is called "uterine vellum."

Parchment is produced by first removing the hair on the animal skins by soaking them for a few days, first in chemicals, and then in water. This softened the skins, allowing workers to scrape off whatever hair remained, and, more importantly, softened the skin so that it could be stretched. And the more the skin was stretched, the thinner it became, making it more suitable as pages for writing. As with papyrus, the surfaces of the raw, stretched skin would be rubbed smooth with a smooth stone or piece of wood. This smoothing is called "pouncing." The pouncing of a surface included the use of a mixture of pastes.

The Cost of an Ancient Bible

I've described the production of papyrus and parchment in some detail because I want to explain the economic cost of ancient writing. The difference between the cost of papyrus and the cost of parchment was enormous. With papyrus plants readily available in Egypt, and Egyptians having highly developed skills in producing papyrus, the cost of papyrus sheets was relatively inexpensive.

The cost of producing parchment made of vellum—uterine vellum in particular—was a different matter. In taking an unborn calf for its skin to produce uterine vellum, the owner lost the potential income from that baby cow or bull. If the unborn calf was female, this economic loss would include, for example, the loss of the potential milk. If the taken calf was male, it meant the economic loss of the siring capacity of the bull. Future offspring were no longer a possibility.

How many vellum sheets could be produced from the skin of an unborn calf? Typically, a calf could produce three or four sheets. These sheets would be folded if the parchment was destined for a codex (book), once for a large book and twice for a smaller book. A sheet folded once yielded four sides or pages for writing. A sheet folded twice yielded eight pages for writing. These folded sheets would be collected with others and sewn together to form a quire, a collection of twenty-four sheets of the same size. Then the quires would be sewn together and bound to form a book. A very rough estimate, based on the number of pages in a modern edition of the Christian Bible, is that the complete ancient Bible of both the Old and the New Testaments would be about 1,500 pages. This means it would take the skins of about forty-seven calves to produce the amount of vellum sheets needed to produce one complete Christian Bible. That's a lot of livestock.

The cost of the materials was not all that went into the budget for producing an ancient Bible. The professional scribe had to be paid. This cost was determined by the number of lines copied. In the year AD 301, by imperial decree, the cost was set at 25 denarii for one hundred lines of "first quality" writing.[1] Based on this rate, it has been computed that a complete Christian Bible, with no illumination—decorative drawing or fancy lettering—would cost about 30,000 denarii. We know from an earlier text from circa AD 215 that a soldier's wages (a legionary—a low-level soldier, the rank equivalent to that of a private or lower) for one year was about 750 denarii.[2] That would mean that one Bible produced around the year AD 300 would cost about forty years of a soldier's wages!

It is extremely difficult to compare the value of ancient Roman money to today's dollar value. But we can make some reasonable comparisons. We know that one denarius was generally a day's wage for an unskilled Roman worker. Think of a day's wage for the lowest unskilled work in the United States today that excludes all typical salary deductions; for example, just the actual money someone might pay the neighbor kid to mow the lawn. With these considerations in mind, that would put the value of a Roman denarius at about twenty dollars. That would mean that a hand-copied, complete Bible could cost well over a half-million dollars in today's money! Just imagine. Making such estimates is a very risky enterprise because of the almost infinite number of variables involved in comparing the value of an ancient coin to monetary values in today's economy. Regardless of any and all such considerations, one can safely say that an ancient Bible, on the best vellum, would cost an immense fortune.

Saving Space on a Page

Why all this calculation? Understanding how very valuable high-quality vellum was and how expensive books were to produce helps us to understand one of the most surprising things about these ancient books. The text of ancient books had no word breaks! There were no spaces between the words! Why? Probably to cram as many letters as possible onto the page to reduce the number of very expensive parchment sheets needed to produce the book. Also in the interest of saving the very valuable real estate on a sheet of vellum, common words that were repeated often (e.g., Lord, Jesus, Christ, Israel, Jerusalem, heaven) were abbreviated. These abbreviated words were usually marked with a symbol, indicating to the reader that the letters represented an abbreviated word.

If you have viewed religious icons, you have probably already seen this phenomenon. For example, with an icon of Jesus Christ you will often see, to the left of Jesus' head, two Greek letters, ις, the first and last letters of the Greek name of Jesus (ιησους) with two horizontal lines over the two letters (the top line often has a little semicircle in the middle of it). Then to the right side of Jesus' head, another two Greek letters: χς, the first and last letters of the Greek word for "Christ" (χριστος). These also usually have the same two lines above them.

Icons of Mary often have similar abbreviations flanking her face. Most often they are μρ, the first and last letters of ματηρ (the Greek word for "mother") on the left side and the two letters θυ, the first and last letters of θεου (the Greek word for "God's") on the right side. Hence, the abbreviations read "God's Mother."

As if all this did not save *enough* space on the page, ancient writing also had no punctuation! There were no commas and no periods to end a sentence or capital letters to signal the beginning of a new sentence. There was no indentation to indicate a new paragraph. These practices were true for both Greek and Hebrew Bibles. But Hebrew writing had even more surprises.

Missing Vowels, Spacing, and Punctuation

Ancient Hebrew (like modern Israeli Hebrew) had no vowels! That's right—no written vowels! Of course, Hebrew speakers *pronounce* vowels when they speak or read from the page, but the vowels are not written. So imagine what confronts the reader of an ancient page from a Hebrew Bible: long lines of uninterrupted consonants across the whole page. How in the world do readers make sense of what they're looking at?

Let's try to visualize this experience, as best we can, in English. Look at the following English text written without vowels, without word breaks, and without punctuation:

drjhnwntmnwhknwswhtlvsllbtyrgnrskndthghtflpplwhrntl-kydmttbngslssndnfrryhvrndmfrthrmnyrnfryhvnflng-swhtsvrwhnwrprtcnbfrvrhppywllyltmbyrsglr

What in the world does this mean? And how can we derive meaning from—dare I say exegete—this scramble of consonants? The interpreter gets some help by at least inserting word breaks. With this help, the text looks like this:

dr jhn wnt mn wh knws wht lv s ll bt y r gnrs knd thghtfl ppl wh r nt lk y dmt t bng slss nd nfrr y hv rnd m fr thr mn yrn fr y hv n flngs whtsvr whn wr prt cn b frvr hppy wll y lt m b yrs glr

Is this much help? Perhaps, but let's get some more help by now supplying vowels:

> dear john i want a man who knows what love is all about
> you are generous kind thoughtful people who are not like
> you admit to being useless and inferior you have ruined me
> for other men i yearn for you i have no feelings whatsoever
> when were apart i can be forever happy will you let me be
> yours gloria

Aha! Now we've got it. It's a love letter from Gloria to John! So now let's just clean it up a bit simply by adding punctuation— some periods, commas, capital letters, and the like. And here's what we get:

> Dear John,
> I want a man who knows what love is all about. You are
> generous, kind, thoughtful. People who are not like you
> admit to being useless and inferior. You have ruined me for
> other men. I yearn for you. I have no feelings whatsoever
> when we're apart. I can be forever happy. Will you let me be
> yours?
> Gloria

Some of you might now recognize this text. It's made its rounds on the internet for some time. If you've already seen it there, then you'll know that this exact same text can be radically transformed by simply changing the punctuation. Note, nothing else in the previous text has been altered but the punctuation (the commas, periods, capital letters, etc.). Now look at this differently punctuated version:

> Dear John:
> I want a man who knows what love is. All about you are generous, kind, thoughtful people who are not like you. Admit to being useless and inferior. You have ruined me. For other men I yearn. For you I have no feelings whatsoever. When we're apart, I can be forever happy.
> Will you let me be!
> Yours,
> Gloria

Not only is the meaning of the text *different*, but the meaning and intent of the letter is really just the *opposite* of the previous text. The meaning has been completely changed simply by altering the punctuation.

I hope this exercise gives you a little sense of what confronts paleographers ("those who study ancient handwriting") and the other readers of ancient Hebrew biblical manuscripts. Now, lest we get upset that the biblical text could be subject to such widely disparate interpretations, depending on who edits the punctuation or adds the vowels, let's remember that most of the texts of the Old Testament were already very well known and widely memorized by many ancient students of the Old Testament. So most ancient readers of the Bible already knew what the texts of the biblical books said. For many ancient readers, the letters on the parchment or papyrus were simply mnemonic devices, that is, aids to their memory. These readers had little difficulty correctly reading and understanding the ancient page.

It's also important to note that the very important word breaks of the biblical texts were not universally inserted, for the most part, until around the fifteenth century with the advent of the printing press. These first printed Bibles and all of the others up to this day all have their roots in the ancient Hebrew and Greek hand-copied texts.

≺ 9 ≻

What Is the Origin of Biblical Chapters and Verses?

The previous chapter might have left you wondering about two other key additions that are a part of your modern Bible: chapters and verses. It should come as no surprise that the original copies of the Bible had no chapter numbers or verses marked on the pages. Where did these come from? Why were they added?

The most basic answer is that the division of the texts into smaller parts was driven by need or at least by expediency. Think of it like this: If you wanted to find that place in the book of Isaiah where the prophet wrote ". . . the young woman, pregnant and about to bear a son, shall name him Emmanuel," how would you find it? Or, suppose you are engaged with some correspondent with whom you are discussing this famous text. How do you communicate to that person where to find it in the book of Isaiah? You can see how helpful a shared system of subdividing these large books would be. It's easy for us today to locate biblical passages. Anyone in the world can ask us to check Isaiah, chapter 7, verse 14, and, because today all Bibles share the same divisions and subdivisions, we can quickly find the text in question. Not so in antiquity.

From at least the sixth century AD and likely even much earlier, books in the Hebrew Bible were already divided into small sections that looked like verses. These divisions were within larger sections that seemed to be driven by subject or theme. Some Hebrew Bibles also designated divisions of larger sections that were used for a three-year lectionary cycle intended for daily synagogue readings.

The earliest divisions of the various books of the Greek version of the Christian Bible showed up even earlier, as far back as fourth century AD. This division of each book into smaller parts was known by a Greek word that roughly translates as *chapters*. But at this early stage, there was no single system of chapter divisions that was universally used or accepted. One ancient Greek Bible was divided one way, a second another way, a third even differently than the first two, and so on. None of these earliest divisions corresponded to the biblical chapters we have today. Nor did these ancient systems insert numbers into the text to mark the beginning of a new "chapter." Most of these ancient manuscripts merely had a mark in the margin, showing the division. It is thought that many of these systems for dividing the texts corresponded to the need for the cycle of readings used in the Christian liturgy. Thus the readings for the day's liturgy could be marked so the reader would know where to begin and where to stop. However, as noted above, these ancient divisions within the biblical books were not universally used or accepted in all parts of the Christian world.

The chapter divisions present in our Bible today date back to the early thirteenth century. An English Roman Catholic cardinal, Stephen Langton, archbishop of Canterbury—primarily known as an inspiring force for the creation of the *Magna Carta*—improvised the divisions of the Bible into chapters that we have today. Langton had written commentaries on the Old Testament that prompted him to subdivide the biblical books into portions that aided him and his readers in finding the particular texts upon which he was commenting.

Addition of Verses

It was a few centuries after the division of the Bible into chapters that the smaller subdivisions of verses were added. Additional smaller divisions within the Hebrew Bible were added by the tenth century AD. As mentioned with the introduction of chapters, these smaller divisions were also probably intended to aid the reader in the synagogue and were similar to what we'd think of today as a period or indication of a pause at the end of a sentence. These new markings were handed down and included in subsequent handmade copies of the Hebrew Bible. After the invention of the printing press, subsequent copies of printed Hebrew Bibles kept these inserted subdivisions as marks on the pages. Since the Hebrew Bible forms the majority of the Old Testament, when Christian Bibles were being printed, the same dividing marks were originally included in the books of the Old Testament portion of the Christian Bibles.

The New Testament books, which were divided into generally accepted chapters by Cardinal Langton, had verses marked within the chapters in 1555 by another medieval man, a French printer named Robert Estienne. He added them to his edition of the Latin Vulgate. His versification of the chapters of the entire Bible—Old and New Testaments—was widely accepted, copied, and distributed in the thousands of Bibles being produced on the printing press. These are the verses we use today. Imagine trying to find that particular biblical passage I mentioned above—Isaiah 7:14—without the aid of chapters or verses? Further, imagine biblical scholars attempting to reference certain scripture texts for a reader or audience without these references. It would be almost impossible.

Another Tool for Scripture Study:
A Concordance

You can probably guess that finding particular words within the Bible is a great part of the foundational work of biblical scholars. We often ask questions like: "What does this word mean? What other biblical writers used this word? How did they use it? Where else in the Bible is the word found?" You can't even begin to address such questions if you can't find all the occurrences of the word within the biblical text. And think of the readers of the scholarly biblical commentaries trying to follow the argument or observations about significant words or phrases, or quotations that are being cited. How could they follow what the biblical scholar is writing about if they too can't find the exact location of the word that is being referenced?

There *is* a very handy tool worth mentioning for locating specific words or phrases in the Bible. It is called a *concordance*. This is a large book (or smart phone app!) that contains *every* word used in the Bible in alphabetical order. There are English concordances for Bibles in English and French concordances for French translations and Greek and Hebrew concordances for the biblical books in their original languages. These concordances show the reader at a glance the chapter and verse where any particular word is found and how many times it occurs in any given book and in the whole Bible. Thank goodness for Cardinal Langton's chapters and Robert Estienne's verses! Thank goodness for the biblical concordance!

So what do you say? Do you think you have a greater knowledge of some of the principles of scripture study? We've looked at a definition of the Bible and how it is a book of inspired truth without error. We've examined some of the tools of scripture study, including the widely encompassing historical-critical method. We've introduced the importance of the geographical location of Israel as a place to encounter a wide variety of foreign cultures that impacted the authors of the Bible and what they wrote. We've also shared an overview of how the Bible was recorded and organized.

I believe you are ready to undertake one of the most fascinating elements of scripture study: to understand how words found in the Bible were understood *when they were written*, before the words and texts became privileged or made "special" by religious beliefs. Studying the original meanings of biblical words is a fascinating process and the subject of part II!

PART II

Scripture Scholarship:

LET'S SAMPLE THE BIBLE'S ORIGINAL MEANING!

There is an Italian proverb that goes like this: "The translator is a traitor." What is meant by that is the translator robs the reader of the true meaning of a word or phrase. Anyone who is bilingual understands how difficult it is to convey the meaning of a word or phrase from a source language by translating it into another language. At no time is this clearer than when someone tries to translate a joke into a different language. Anyone who has tried this knows that it is all but impossible for the translated joke to have the same impact that it does in its original language.

Words convey multivalent meanings. Yet, there is rarely significant attention paid to the study of the exact intended meaning of key words individually within a sentence or passage. For example, consider if you were not familiar with the small three-letter English word "hit." Think of all the various meanings this individual word has: It can describe a popular song or a Broadway play. It can mean a physical action that inflicts personal injury. It can convey emotional impact. To some, it might mean a drag on a marijuana joint or a shot of alcohol. Nowadays, the word can also mean a visit to a website.

Now try to understand the meaning of words with religious significance, and you have a whole different kettle of fish. (Imagine trying to translate the meaning of the idiom "kettle of fish" into another language!) There are two main languages found in the Bible: Hebrew and Greek. A third language, Aramaic, is found in small portions (for example, in the book of Daniel). Over the centuries, we've invested religious meaning into many of the words in the biblical texts. But originally, many of these same words could not have conveyed the same meanings as they do now. I like to call this later investment of religious meaning into words the "religification" of vocabulary.

All of these linguistic issues come into sharper focus when we talk about encountering Jesus as we come to know him in the New Testament. The gospels give us memories of Jesus, recorded not by the actual eyewitnesses to his words and actions, but by the evangelists who were from the subsequent, later generation. The gospels present some remembered elements of Jesus' life and teaching. Some other elements about Jesus and what he taught are found elsewhere in the New Testament, particularly in the letters of St. Paul.

The difficulties in translating the gospels and the other New Testament writings are, to use a biblical term, *legion*! The job is hampered not only by the extreme age of the texts, but also by the differences and peculiarities of the languages involved. And, perhaps most significantly, the gospels and other New Testament writings are the most privileged, honored, and revered texts in our faith and in western culture. These biblical books are not novels or plays or biographies (though the Bible does contain some of those genres of literature!).

Rather, these texts come to us from God. They contain his inspired truth. When we respond "Thanks be to God" after the lector at Mass ends a reading with "The Word of the Lord" we affirm that this is what we truly believe. So imagine the pressure for a biblical scholar or linguist trying to accurately translate words that come from God into a new, different language.

Knowing the life of Jesus and what his followers believed about him from the words of the New Testament is not an easy task.

In part II, we will look at nine such "religified" themes and accompanying words and phrases that come from the New Testament. Having looked at a specific word or phrase, we will then step back and consider what its origins tell us about Jesus' life, teaching, and meaning. Ultimately, this is the goal of scripture scholarship and biblical study for Christians: to *understand* and follow Jesus' teachings better. Put another way, the central aim of theology and our Catholic Christian faith is to understand the revelation of God the Father in the words and actions of Christ. The record of that revelation and of Christ and his teaching is found in the words of the New Testament.

We are going to follow a loosely chronological path that focuses on themes arranged around the words or phrases connected to the life and ministry of Jesus. Certainly, this list is not exhaustive. Rather, it is designed to help you get a flavor of scripture scholarship using some methods and dealing with some of the issues introduced in part I. A goal is for you to understand what the biblical writers meant when they originally wrote their words and how the original audience understood those words. An even more important goal is for this material to help you deepen your understanding of Jesus and strengthen your faith with this new knowledge.

All of this careful study may spark some controversy. No wonder. Scripture study is a very difficult and complicated endeavor. It is also very rewarding and enriching. So fasten your mental seatbelts and take care to study and pray your way through these topics.

‹ 10 ›

Is "Christ" Jesus' Last Name?

Many people *do* think that "Christ" is Jesus' last name. That is understandable because it appears so very often after the name "Jesus" in the New Testament. But Christ is not his last name. In fact, it is a title and an important one at that.

The origin for the title "Christ" is the Greek noun χριστος (formed from the participle for the Greek verb χριω—"to oil something"). This word is a translation of the Hebrew word *mashah*. The adjective or participle form of this verb is *messiah*, which means "anointed one" or "anointed thing." In ancient Judaism, the anointing of a person was often connected with marking a change in the status of the person or marking him for a new job or office. This type of anointing could have been for a person being called to be a prophet, priest, or for a man being enthroned as a king. In ancient Israel, since the king was the most notable person anointed with oil, the Hebrew participle for "anointed one" generally came to refer to the king of Israel. After the independent monarchy of Israel had passed, the term came to refer to the future promised king who would save Israel. This coming king who was to right ancient wrongs was simply referred to as "the Messiah" or "the Anointed One" by the Jewish people. Around this figure swirled religious hopes of salvation and political hopes for liberation.

There was a glitch with the Greek word χριστος. Rather than being *translated* in our English translations of the Bible, the word was simply *transliterated* from its Greek letters to the Roman letters we use for English and it was capitalized: *C-h-r-i-s-t*. And to make it sound more like an English word, someone dropped that Greek-looking ending -ος (-os). Hence we have *Christ* appearing in our modern Bibles and not Christos (χριστος).

The Greek verb χριω also had the meaning of anointed. It was often used to describe the rubbing of one's body with oil. This was a common way of bathing by the ancient Greeks and Romans. Typically a man would go to the public bathhouses and, while there, he would sweat in a sauna-like heated room, have his body scraped with an instrument called a *strigil*, and then have aromatic oils rubbed on the skin. This was especially practiced by athletes of the time. With the use of this transliterated word χριστος in our Bible, we have a Greek translation of an important Hebrew word, "messiah"; however, this connection to anointing or "being rubbed with oil" is completely lost. More importantly, even the connection between "Christ" and "messiah" is lost. It's worth pointing out that there *are* some familiar modern English nouns that derive from the same word χριστος, including *chrism*, the name for the sacred oil used in the Sacraments of Baptism, Confirmation, and Holy Orders. Even the word *Crisco* of kitchen-product fame also comes from the same Greek word.

The Greek speaker and reader understood immediately that χριστος meant "messiah." And Jesus would be identified with this promised figure—the Messiah—from very early on. The belief among Jesus' followers and Jesus' occasional self-references made it clear to some that he was the yearned-for Messiah. So it is not surprising that Christ became a title for Jesus: "Jesus the Messiah" or "Jesus the Anointed One." In Greek, the phrase is "ιησους ο χριστος," that is, "Jesus the Messiah." Christ is used more than 450 times in the New Testament in connection with Jesus. No wonder folks could think that "Christ" was another name for Jesus or even his last name. But by *transliterating* the

Greek word into Roman letters rather than translating it as "messiah" deprives the English reader of that important and oft-repeated belief of early Christians—that Jesus *was* the Messiah!

Here's an exercise to help you remember that Christ is a title, not a name, for Jesus. In your mind, verbally replace all the 450 or so instances of the word "Christ" in the New Testament with the word "Messiah." If you do, you begin to get the message very clearly that Jesus *is* the Messiah, the Anointed One! Furthermore, since this title is so often applied to Jesus in the New Testament, it also becomes very apparent that his first followers thought this to be a very important aspect of Jesus' identity, an aspect clear to ancient readers but not as clear to us today.

≺ 11 ≻

Where Did Jesus Come From?

Here at the seminary, where I teach, I've become infamous for my questions concerning Bethlehem as the historical birthplace of Jesus. I endure endless ribbing at Christmastime. Students will start singing "O Little Town of Bethlehem" when I walk by. My fellow priests on the faculty will turn around and give me a long stare and slight nod from the sanctuary whenever Bethlehem as Jesus' birthplace comes up during a homily. They're all in on the joke. So I must admit at the outset that it's true: I am one of the biblical professors who questions the historical accuracy (*note*: not theological truth!) of the Lord's birth in Bethlehem.

Surprisingly, there is a lot of evidence to support such doubts about the historicity of the accounts of Jesus' birth in the Gospels of Matthew and Luke. I'm certainly not alone among Catholic biblical scholars who doubt or outright deny Jesus' birthplace in Bethlehem. Fr. Raymond Brown, Fr. Joseph Fitzmyer, S.J., and Fr. John Meier are only a few of the more prominent scholars among them. Even Pope Benedict XVI mentions the controversy surrounding Jesus' birthplace, in passing, in his 2012 book *Jesus of Nazareth: The Infancy Narratives*, focusing particularly on questions of the "worldwide census" (see Luke 2:1) that drew the Holy Family to Bethlehem. Pope Benedict is aware of some questions regarding this issue, but wishes to focus instead on larger theological points about the account of Jesus' birth. He wrote: "There is a long-running dispute among experts regarding this tax collection (population census), but there is no need for us to enter into all the details here."[1]

As for me, for some years I kept my scholarly skepticism about the historical accuracy of Bethlehem as Jesus' birthplace private. I knew that expressing my opinions and exegetical concerns would stir up strong emotions. But I continued my study and research, deepening my understanding of the exegetical issues surrounding this question. When I decided to share what I had learned, I quickly realized that I had to do so very carefully because many people have very strong feelings about this topic. Later, after I'd decided to start opening up about this study and speak of it with parishioners and students, I saw firsthand the reactions it caused. And it is this strong, emotional response to the issue that I want to address at the outset.

It is difficult for us to realize how deeply our thinking is influenced by images, memories, and traditions. Think of all the Christmas cards, the crèche scenes set before our Christmas trees, the Christmas plays we were in or we watched as children, the religious movies, and on and on. And don't forget the Christmas music! It would take a page to list the lyrics of Christmas carols that include references to Bethlehem. I might add, too, that many of them include mention of deep snow and freezing temperatures. And while snow in Bethlehem is not unknown, it was and remains a rarity. We've been inundated with these Christmas traditions since we were children, while at the same time struggling to stay awake to witness the arrival of Santa Claus on Christmas Eve!

Because of our personal and cultural Christmas memories, it is easy to understand the resistance many of us feel when we consider the possibility that Jesus was not born in Bethlehem. But we must admit that these embedded images do not come from our study or analysis of the biblical texts. They come from the cultural extras that surround the celebration of one of the most favorite feast days of the liturgical *and* civil year.

So I do ask you, as we continue this discussion about Jesus' birthplace, to acknowledge how much your thoughts of Christmas are influenced by your own cultural traditions, many of which are emotionally charged. My second request is that, at least for the moment, you set aside such influences so that we can more clearly assess the scholarly work on this question from the gospel texts themselves.

So let's get to the actual texts of the infancy narratives to catch you up with some of my research.

The Infancy Narratives Are in Two Gospels

Only the gospels of Matthew (1:18–2:23) and Luke (2:1–40) include the infancy narratives of Jesus. It is only a guess as to when these gospels were written. I generally date Matthew between AD 85 and 90 and Luke a bit later, around AD 90–100. Both of these infancy narratives concern more than just the actual birth of Jesus. Matthew's version, for example, includes the Holy Family's flight to Egypt, the murder of the Holy Innocents, and the Holy Family's return from Egypt after the death of Herod the Great. Luke's version mentions none of this.

Any comparison of the two versions of Jesus' birth makes it clear that these are two very different accounts. This suggests that there was not a single, older account that Matthew's and Luke's versions were based on. Instead, it likely means that two oral accounts of Jesus' infancy developed independently of each other and were handed down separately. The wide variance between the two accounts also suggests that neither could be based on any historical, eyewitness memories of the events. If they were, one would expect to find some overlap of at least some elements of the accounts that agree with each other. Yet other than the town of Bethlehem, these stories have almost nothing in common. Let's take a look at each gospel's version separately.

Taking a Closer Look at the Infancy Narrative in Matthew's Gospel

Matthew's infancy narrative (Mt 1:18–2:23) does not mention a census or any travel of Mary and Joseph before Jesus was born. The annunciation, or announcement of Jesus' birth, is in a dream to Joseph (not to Mary), and it presumably happens in Bethlehem of Judea.

There is no account of Joseph and Mary seeking shelter and being turned away from an inn in Matthew's gospel. There is no mention of a manger or the suggestions of an animal stall or cave as the place of the birth, as we find in Luke. Since the gospel assumes that Joseph lives in Bethlehem, the presumption is that Mary gave birth in Joseph's home in Bethlehem. If this were so, then Joseph's home would also be the place where the magi came to do homage to Jesus. And, perhaps Jesus was not an infant, but up to two years old, the upper age of male children ordered to death by Herod. Note how Matthew describes Herod's command: "He ordered the massacre of all the boys in Bethlehem and its vicinity two years old and younger, in accordance with the time he ascertained from the magi" (Mt 2:16).

Only Matthew mentions the flight into Egypt that was prompted by the murderous rampage of Herod the Great. At the end of the Holy Family's stay in Egypt, Matthew says that Joseph initially planned to return to Judea, suggesting again that he had a home there. (Bethlehem is in Judea, a very near suburb of Jerusalem.) But "he was afraid to go back there. And because he had been warned in a dream, he departed for the region of Galilee. He went and dwelt in a town called Nazareth" (Mt 2:22–23). Oddly, the text states that Joseph avoided Judea because of Herod's son, Archelaus, who was ruling there but then moves the family to Galilee where Herod's other son, Antipas, was reigning. This is curious, to say the least, for as Fr. John Meier points out, this kingdom of Herod Antipas is where "the future slayer of John the Baptist, is ruling! Out of the frying pan into the fire. Joseph has a strange sense of security measures."[2]

Is There Support for Matthew's Infancy Narrative Elsewhere in the Bible?

Briefly put, there is no collaboration of the details found in Matthew's infancy account anyplace else within the Bible, and not even within *his own gospel*. Both Matthew and Luke agree in their otherwise divergent infancy accounts that Jesus was not raised in the south, the area of Judea, but in the north, the region of Galilee, in the village of Nazareth. Matthew 13:54 states, referring to Nazareth, that Jesus "came to his native place and taught the people in their synagogue." The rest of that verse and the ones that follow (vv. 55–58) give an account of a crowd's reaction to him that clearly affirms that they believe Jesus and his parents are natives of Galilee. Matthew 4:13 and 9:1 also locate Jesus' home as being Capernaum in the north, in Galilee, and note that his public ministry took place there.

Is There Support for Matthew's Infancy Narrative outside the Bible?

Looking at Matthew's version, we see elements that beg for support from historical data outside the Bible, including mention of a rising star that led the magi and the wide-scale murder of male children so near to the famous provincial capital Jerusalem. Each of these events should have left some notice in non-Christian historical records.

Regarding the star noted in Matthew 2:2, there have been attempts by planetariums across the world to turn back the celestial clock, as they can do, to re-create the stars and their positions in the heavens on any given date in history. There are also ancient records of significant astronomical events in history. For example, an appearance of Halley's Comet is dated back to 240 BC. Its appearance was also noted in 12 BC. Certainly, Halley's Comet would have been in view of the entire ancient world. But the dating is off for connecting any such appearance with Jesus' birth. The year 12 BC is much earlier than any credible scholarship dates the birth of Jesus.

There was also a rare conjunction of planetary appearances that occurred in the early summer and early and late fall in 7 BC. Jupiter and Saturn were conjoined in appearance within the zodiac sign of Pisces. This is a phenomenon that occurs every 257 years on average. But we don't know how this phenomenon might have been interpreted by ancient Romans, Jews, or Persians at the time. (Persia was the reputed homeland of the magi.) It was only centuries later that some biblical scholars working with astronomers attributed this celestial anomaly to the "star of Bethlehem." Yet there were no contemporary historical witnesses to this sighting or any interpretation of the conjunction of the planets (note planets, *not* stars) Jupiter and Saturn in any historical record.[3] It is accurate to say that while many attempts have presented provocative results, showing peculiar *and notable* celestial anomalies, none can be tagged to any of the nights around the postulated date of Jesus' birth.

I think even more telling is that there are no non-biblical accounts of the "massacre of all the boys in Bethlehem and its vicinity two years old and under" (Mt 2:16). Again, I must point out that Bethlehem is only five miles from Jerusalem, the provincial capital, and reachable on foot in less than an hour. Such a slaughter of children, so near the city of Jerusalem, surely would have been remembered and recorded in some documents. Even our most important extra-biblical, historical witness of this period, Flavius Josephus, who elsewhere displays antipathy for Herod the Great, writes nothing about this slaughter. This is surprising because Josephus contemptuously tells us of other atrocities committed by Herod the Great: the murder of his wife, the killing of his sons (his oldest, he killed shortly before his death), and his posthumous order that several prominent Jewish leaders be murdered at the time of his death simply to ensure that *someone* would be weeping during his funeral! It seems impossible that Josephus would have made no comment on *this* heinous crime of the killing of babies in Bethlehem ordered by Herod.

Taking a Closer Look at the Infancy Narrative in Luke's Gospel

Now let's look at the infancy narrative from Luke 1:5–2:52. In this account, the angel's announcement of the birth of Jesus is to Mary, not Joseph (1:26–38). Mary's hometown—and by implication the hometown of her betrothed, Joseph—is "a town of Galilee called Nazareth" (1:26). Prior to the birth of Jesus, Mary travels south, into Judea, to "a town of Judah" (1:39) to visit Elizabeth, who was pregnant with John the Baptist. At the end of her visit of about three months, Mary "returned to her home" (1:56), already identified as Nazareth. Later in her pregnancy, Mary travels with Joseph a second time from their home in Nazareth south to Judea, but this time to Bethlehem in order for Joseph to register in the census (2:4). Why Joseph would have his very pregnant wife accompany him for this arduous trip is never mentioned by Luke. On the face of it, it would seem odd for Joseph to put his wife through this.

There are also several unique details in Luke's account around the actual birth of Jesus. There is an appearance of "the angel of the Lord" to "shepherds in that region living in the fields and keeping the night watch over their flock" (2:8–9). Did anyone else see this appearance? If not, why not? After finding the new-born child, the shepherds "made known the message that had been told them about this child" (2:17) and they glorified and praised God for "all they had heard and seen, just as it had been told to them" (2:20). We must consider here that if the shepherds had indeed made this message known to others, why wouldn't others have remembered and recounted what the shepherds told them? But we have no historical record of the appearance of an angel nor of the shepherds' accounts.

Luke's infancy narrative also extends past Jesus' birth. Luke 2:22–38 tells of the Holy Family traveling to the Temple in Jerusalem for Mary's purification and to offer the required sacrifice for a firstborn male child. While they are there, two people appear: an elderly man named Simeon and a prophetess named Anna. Both are immediately aware of the importance of the child Jesus and praise God when they see him. Anna then begins to speak "about the child to all who were awaiting the redemption of Jerusalem" (Lk 2:38).

The infancy narrative in Luke's gospel ends with Jesus' return to the Temple as a twelve-year-old boy. It is not clear in Luke if this trip to Jerusalem included Jesus' bar mitzvah, typically celebrated for boys of that age, or if it is at the time of Passover, as it is mentioned that "each year his parents went to Jerusalem for the feast of the Passover" (2:41). Jesus remained behind in Jerusalem without his parents. When they returned after three days, they "found him in the temple, sitting in the midst of the teachers, listening to them and asking them questions, and all who heard him were amazed at his answers" (2:46-47).

In Luke's infancy narrative, there are a lot of people who saw or heard about Jesus' birth in Bethlehem and his display of knowledge as a boy of twelve at the Temple in Jerusalem.

And yet later in Luke's gospel there is little or no memory of these amazing events, nor are there any extra-biblical historical memories of them.

Is There Support for Luke's Infancy Narrative Elsewhere in the Bible?

Luke's gospel depicts so many events of Jesus' earliest life as very public that one wonders how it is possible that these events seem to have been forgotten by everyone, even later, within Luke's own gospel—let alone within the other three gospel accounts and the rest of the New Testament!

In comparing Matthew's infancy narrative with Luke's, it is clear there are significant differences. Remember that the only common element in the two accounts is that both Matthew and Luke name Jesus' birthplace as Bethlehem. Matthew's infancy narrative makes no mention of the census that is the reason for the travel to Bethlehem mentioned in Luke's gospel. And, outside the infancy narratives in both gospels, Bethlehem is *never again* referred to as Jesus' birthplace. The other two gospels—Mark and John—do not mention any details of Jesus' birth. The Acts of the Apostles—written as a second part to Luke's gospel by the same author—shares no more information about Jesus' birth. The New Testament letters do not make reference to the events described in either infancy narrative.

Indeed, on the contrary, within the New Testament, Jesus is *never* referred to as someone from Bethlehem or Judea (the region where Bethlehem was located). Jesus is *only* referred to as a Galilean or a Nazorean; that is, someone from the north, the region of Galilee or specifically, from the town of Nazareth. Even the Gospel of Matthew's infancy narrative ends with a prophecy that touts his residence in Nazareth: "He shall be called a Nazorean" (Mt 2:23). The Greek word to describe Jesus'

hometown in Matthew's gospel is πατρις (Mt 13:54). Some
English versions translate this word as "his own country," or "his
native place." Combined with the other references in Matthew
that label Jesus as a Nazorean, it is clear that πατρις ("country"
or "native place"), for Matthew, refers to Nazareth, not to Bethlehem. The Gospel of Mark uses this word πατρις twice (Mk 6:1;
4). The first time refers to Nazareth and the second time Jesus
uses the word to quote a proverb of sorts, that "a prophet is not
without honor except in his native place." In Mark's gospel, Jesus
is later referred to several times as being from Nazareth (e.g. Mk
10:47, 14:67, and 16:6). The Gospel of John has no information
about Jesus' birth in Bethlehem and John consistently refers to
Jesus as "Jesus of Nazareth" (e.g., Jn 18:5, 18:7, 19:19).

In a scene from John's gospel, while Jesus is teaching in the
Temple, his hearers speculate about whether he could possibly
be the Messiah: "Others said, 'This is the Messiah.' But others
said, 'The Messiah will not come from Galilee, will he? Does not
scripture say that the Messiah will be of David's family and come
from Bethlehem, the village where David lived?'" (Jn 7:41–42).
Wouldn't this be the perfect opportunity for someone to remember and shout, "In fact, this man *is* a Judean! He *was* born in
Bethlehem!" But not a word is mentioned. No one contradicts
what is being said. John's gospel clearly believes Jesus is a Galilean and from Nazareth.

The Gospel of Luke, itself, states later, about Jesus: "He came
to Nazareth, where he had grown up" (Lk 4:16). It is possible to
take this to mean that while he was born elsewhere (in Bethlehem) as Luke states, he came "back to" or "returned to" Nazareth.
However, Luke (as do the other gospels) refers repeatedly to
Jesus as "Jesus of Nazareth" in other places (e.g., Lk 4:34, 18:37,
24:19).

This absence of any references to Jesus being from Bethlehem or Judea in any place in the gospels besides the two infancy
narratives is remarkable because it would have been in the interest of Jesus and his followers that he be known as a man from

Bethlehem, as the above example from John suggests. There is an Old Testament reference from the prophet Micah that the Messiah would be born in Bethlehem (see Micah 5:2). Any claims made by Jesus himself or by his followers that Jesus was the longed-for Messiah would have been bolstered by evidence or memories that he really was born in Bethlehem. And yet no evidence of this is offered except—and *only*—in the infancy narratives of Matthew and Luke.

Is There Support for Luke's Infancy Narrative outside the Bible?

Unlike Matthew's, Luke's version alludes to only a few events connected to Jesus' birth that would necessarily spark comment or be remembered in non-biblical, historical sources. One could consider the appearance of the angels and a heavenly host in the skies over Bethlehem a "cosmic event," observable and memorable by others, but no extra-biblical sources mention such an event. More noteworthy at the time would seem to be the "decree" that "went out from Caesar Augustus that the world should be enrolled" in a census of some kind (Lk 2:1). This was the reason Luke gave for Joseph taking his family from the town of Nazareth in Galilee all the way to Bethlehem in Judea. While Luke does not specifically state the reason for the imperial registration, it is safely assumed he's referring to a census being taken for tax or military reasons, as was typical for Roman administration.

While there is evidence of Roman tax records from censuses being done in various provinces or cities of the empire, there is no historical account of an empire-wide census taking place during the reign of Caesar Augustus. Furthermore, there is no record of the empire requiring taxpayers to register in the place of their birth. Rather the common practice was that a taxpayer would register to pay his taxes only at the place where he owned property. The only census for which there is historical evidence was a provincial census for the province of Syria, whose governor was then Quirinius. This provincial census is mentioned by the ancient Jewish historian, Flavius Josephus, who also dated it at AD 6. But we have to wonder if this is the census referred to by Luke. And, if it *was* AD 6, then Jesus was hardly a newborn baby at the time. In *Jesus of Nazareth: The Infancy Narratives*, Pope Benedict explained this discrepancy by saying ancient censuses took a very long time to complete. If Jesus' birth is correctly dated as 5 BC at the latest (Jesus was born while Herod the Great was king of Judea and we know that Herod the Great died in 4 BC) this provincial census of Syria would have taken more than eleven years to complete. This *is* possible, but not likely.

Where does Jesus come from? While this will remain a much-disputed question beyond this discussion, the answer is: historically speaking, Jesus was probably not born in Bethlehem. Nowhere in the New Testament is Jesus ever called a Judean or a Bethlehemite—though in many ways, it would have been to Jesus' advantage to be known as a Judean or a Bethlehemite. I suggest both here and to my students that Jesus was probably born in the village of Nazareth in Galilee, the northern region of Israel, not in the southern region of Judea where Bethlehem is located. And this is the reason that my students and faculty peers often tease me around the Christmas holiday!

So *Why* Do Matthew and Luke Tell Us That Jesus Was Born in Bethlehem?

The question that heads this section can be answered in one word: theology. The gospels were not written as historical documents. The writers of the gospels were not modern historians or historians at all. What we expect to find in a historical account we simply will not find in the gospels of Matthew and Luke or in any gospel or even in *any* biblical book. While there is accurate historical data to be found in the New Testament, the New Testament is *not* a historical work but a theological work.

To help us understand this, let's consider more about the process of writing the gospels. The memories of Jesus' life expanded and developed as his original followers told and retold their stories. After the deaths of the eyewitnesses to Jesus' life, those in the next generation continued to expand and develop the stories and eventually wrote them down. They also organized and rearranged random stories into a more cohesive whole. The opening of Luke's gospel says so: "Since many have undertaken to compile a narrative of the events that have been fulfilled among us, just as those who were eyewitnesses from the beginning and ministers of the word have handed them down to us, I too have decided, after investigating everything accurately anew, to write it down in an orderly sequence for you" (Lk 1:1–3). Luke seems to be critiquing the other written accounts as *not* being in the order that he preferred and not in the order that he finally chose for *his* gospel.

Also, remember the primary reason Luke and the other evangelists undertook writing a narrative of Jesus' life. It certainly was not to give biographical data. The first followers of Jesus and those who heard their eyewitness testimony had soul-shaking, personal encounters with Jesus—the risen Jesus—an encounter that they wished to replicate for others so that others could have the same life-changing contact with the risen Lord that they had. Just imagine the impressions made upon the disciples of Jesus as they were present with him through his ministry, at the time of his suffering and death, and especially as witnesses to his Resurrection. What an impact such events must have had on them!

Even more to the point: What media were available to these first disciples to enable them to transmit the impact Jesus had on them to others who had not met him in person? Their media choices were limited to two: speaking and writing. First they told

the stories orally, especially in their preaching. The generation
that followed the first disciples was the one who eventually put
the good news of these life-changing events into writing. These
were the gospels.

With this perspective in mind, we need to look at what was
the primary concern about Jesus that those early preachers and,
eventually, the gospel writers wanted to convey. In fact, one of
the primary concerns was that people understand *that Jesus
was the promised Messiah of Judaism.* The Jewish expectations
of who this Messiah would be and what he would be like varied
widely in details. Some thought the coming Messiah would be
a great prophet like Elijah. Others thought the Messiah would
be a military figure, like King David or Judas Maccabaeus. Some
thought of the Messiah as a priestly figure who would return the
priesthood and the cult of the Temple to their proper sanctity.
Many thought the Messiah would be a descendant of David,
a man of the Davidic dynasty who would restore the Davidic
monarchy and rule from Jerusalem. All of these expectations
had their roots in the Hebrew scriptures.

Noting the wide variety of expectations of the Messiah from
Jewish tradition and scripture, we need to remember a more
essential point: All the first Christians did indeed believe Jesus
was the Messiah (recall how often the Greek title χριστος is used
throughout the New Testament), however different their expectations and ideas about the Messiah might have been. If we were
to gather up all these various expectations of the Messiah and
put them all into one bag, that bag was tied to Jesus. I think of
it as the transitive property of equality I learned in freshman
year algebra or in intro to logic: If $x = y$ and $y = z$ than $x = z$. In
other words, if "what you think the Messiah is" equals "x" and
"x" equals "Jesus," then "Jesus is what you think the Messiah is."
And if one of the things you think about the Messiah is that he
has to be born in Bethlehem (cf. Mi 5:1), then your messianic
thinking *must* include that Jesus was born in Bethlehem. Let me
explain further.

Let's say that you were raised Jewish before becoming a Christian. You have recently learned about Jesus and have come to believe he is the Messiah. Next, taking everything you thought and learned about the Messiah while being raised Jewish, you now apply *that* to what you believe about Jesus. I know this seems simplistic, but then recall the wide variety of things that Jews thought about what the Messiah would be like: He would be a prophet like Elijah. He would be a military revolutionary who would liberate Jews from Roman oppression. He would be a new high priest. He would be a descendant of David who would restore the Davidic dynasty and rule from Jerusalem. So, if you believed that Jesus was the Messiah, then you believed that not only is Jesus the one predicted by your Jewish ancestors, but he is also the one who fits some or all of those messianic elements.

Now let's add a totally different perspective. Suppose you're a Roman Gentile who knows nothing about this Jewish figure, the Messiah. How did the early followers of Jesus preach to a *gentile* community and explain that Jesus is the Messiah? These folks had never even heard the word *messiah*, much less understood anything about Elijah, the prophets, King David, and all the rest. So the early preachers to Gentiles would first have to explain all sorts of things about Judaism, including all this background information concerning the figure of the Messiah. This would have been needed before they could go on to explain that Jesus *is* that Messiah.

However these first preachers explained the meaning of messiah, we do know that they did it immediately. Naming Jesus as the Messiah was one of the first things shared about Jesus. One simple confirmation of this, remember, is that the Greek translation of messiah—χριστος (the Christ)—was attached to Jesus in the earliest written records of the first Christians, the letters of St. Paul. For example, in the oldest piece of New Testament writing, the First Letter to the Thessalonians (ca. AD 48), Paul refers to Jesus as "the Christ" eleven different times. This is an indication that teaching that "Jesus is the Christ—the

Messiah" was essential and established early. Be aware, also, that Paul's audience in ancient Thessalonica was primarily a gentile, Greco-Roman audience.

How Beliefs about the Messiah Impacted the Infancy Narratives

Now back to Bethlehem. As mentioned previously, one thing that most Jews believed about the Messiah was that whoever he would be, he *had* to be born in Bethlehem, as stated in the book of Micah:

> But you, Bethlehem-Ephrathah
> > least among the clans of Judah,
> From you shall come forth for me
> > one who is to be ruler in Israel;
> Whose origin is from of old
> > from ancient times. (5:1)

We are reminded of this prophecy in Matthew's infancy narrative where Herod summons his advisors and asks them where the Messiah was to be born: "They said to him, 'In Bethlehem of Judea'" (Mt 2:5). Matthew then quotes the Old Testament verse from Micah 5:1. Think again how this relates to the transitive property of equality: if you came to believe that Jesus is the Messiah, then you also believed that Jesus *had to have been* born in Bethlehem.

Such beliefs about the Messiah and beliefs about Jesus take us out of the realm of modern historiography and into the realm of theology, religion, and faith. Precisely how and when this messianic theology became an integral part of the oral traditions about Jesus is unclear; we can only say, as suggested above, it was *very* early and widespread in the Church's history.

The Theology of the Infancy Narratives

When the oral versions of the various gospels were finally written down, the writers wrote *what they believed*. These writers, while contributing their own literary skills in recording the stories and developing the outline of their accounts, did not make things up. They were not so innovative with regard to content.[4] Luke is rather explicit about this. He states that he too decided "after investigating everything anew, to write it down in an orderly sequence for you" (Lk 1:33). These are items he knew well from hearing the oral accounts of the gospel repeated so often. But he also tells us that he believes his account confirms "the certainty of the teachings you have received" (Lk 1:4). In other words, Luke's audience *already knows* what he writes about Jesus, though they may have known an account that presented a different "sequence" of events.

We can assume, then, that both Matthew and Luke believed that Jesus *was* born in Bethlehem and they assumed that their readers already believed this as well. This means that the infancy narratives had already come together as part of the oral tradition, albeit later than the other oral traditions behind the gospels. For both Matthew and Luke, Jesus' birth in Bethlehem helps their audience to understand and affirm that Jesus *was* the Messiah.

Both Matthew's and Luke's infancy narratives are symbolic, compressed versions of each of their gospels. The infancy narratives anticipate, each in their own way, what is to follow in their gospels, and in the case of Luke, not only in his gospel, but also in his second volume, Acts of the Apostles. And what is anticipated in what follows the infancy narratives in Matthew and Luke is basically the reaction to the preaching of the gospel itself. As the world and persons reacted to the birth of Jesus in the infancy narratives, so persons and the world would later react to Jesus himself and to the gospel he preached.

Scripture scholar Fr. Raymond Brown explains that Matthew's infancy narrative presents three reactions to the revelation of God in Christ. Joseph is described as a just, Torah-observant Jew who accepts the word of God given to him by the angel in his dream. He accepts what he hears and is obedient. The magi, Gentiles from far away, follow God's revelation from nature (the star), and they get close. They arrive in Jerusalem. But the revelation from nature is not quite enough. They must consult the Jewish scriptures, and upon learning from the book of the prophet Micah that the Messiah was to be born in nearby Bethlehem, they make their way to the newborn babe and they worship him and offer him gifts. But Herod and the chief priests and the scribes, although they know the Messiah has been born, do not accompany the magi to worship him. Quite the contrary; they seek to murder the child.

The same reactions to Jesus and his message occur in the rest of the Gospel of Matthew. Some Gentiles eagerly become followers of Jesus. Some righteous Jews, like Joseph, are open to new revelations from God, as witnessed by Joseph's reaction to his "annunciation" dream. Matthew's gospel praises the scribe who can combine the new with the old (see Matthew 13:52). Herod, the chief priests, and the scribes who consult the scriptures in the infancy narrative represent those Jewish leaders and the Gentile ruler Pilate who will later put Jesus to death. And, by implication, these same three reactions affected the early preachers of the gospel after Jesus' Ascension. The same reaction will subsequently also affect the readers of the gospel. Some Jews will see the light of Christ and follow it, other Jews will oppose and persecute the early Christians, and some early Christians will suffer greatly at the hands of Gentile Roman rulers.

Brown draws similar conclusions concerning the infancy narrative in comparison to the rest of Luke's gospel and to the Acts of the Apostles. In the Temple, the aged Simeon predicts that the child Jesus will be the cause of the rise and fall of many in Israel and that he will be opposed. Luke also presents those like Zechariah, the shepherds, Simeon and the prophetess Anna who eagerly accept the revelation of God in Christ. In Luke's infancy narrative, these events surrounding Jesus' birth foreshadow what will happen to Mary, to the adult Jesus, and to Jesus' followers after his Ascension. The sword that was predicted to pierce her heart alludes to the later sufferings of Jesus, as well as to the sufferings of his first disciples, Paul, and others in the early Church who will suffer for their acceptance and preaching of the good news.[5]

In conclusion, it is for theological reasons that Jesus is born in Bethlehem, not for historical reasons. The theological agenda of both gospel writers help us to understand why these infancy narratives are included. Knowing this theological thinking of Matthew and Luke helps us to know the Jesus that *they* knew and the *religious truth* of their teaching that Jesus *was* the Messiah and therefore had to have been born in Bethlehem.

≺ 12 ≻

How Is Our Understanding of Baptism Derived from Scripture?

I'm placing the discussion of baptism here, following the chapter of Jesus' birth and origins, because the synoptic gospels all mention that Jesus was baptized by John the Baptist just prior to the beginning of his public ministry (in Matthew 3:1–17, Mark 1:2–8, and Luke 3:2–17). While I'll touch on Jesus' baptism in this chapter, I also plan to delve deeper into other mentions of baptism in scripture (and in some non-biblical sources as well) in order to help us trace the roots of this practice. St. Paul writes significantly on baptism, connecting this ritual action to a saving one while explaining that baptism facilitates our dying to an old life and being "resurrected" to a new life. Let's begin.

The Meaning of "Baptize" prior to the New Testament

Words in the original Greek of the New Testament and the original Hebrew of the Old Testament often had a different meaning or feel than the English words we've used to translate them. This is true for the word *baptism* and some of its derivatives. In fact, the English word "baptize" is not really an English word at all. It is a neologism, that is, a new, made-up word. The word baptize we use in English is really just the Greek word βαπτιζω that has been transliterated using Roman letters and given the English verb ending "-ize."

Most people today—Christian and non-Christian alike—understand "baptize" or "baptism" to mean the ritual used in Christian churches to initiate new members. Depending on our experience of this ritual, the word can mean a few drops of water sprinkled over the head of an infant who is held over a baptismal basin or font, or it could conjure images of adults in white garments standing chest high in the waters of a river or creek with a minister plunging them down below the surface. In fact, if Christians didn't apply the word *baptism* to both such rituals, one could imagine that an uninformed observer of both actions would never guess that the act of pouring a few drops of water on the head of an ornately dressed baby in the baptistery of a church could possibly have anything to do with pushing fully grown adults down into the waters of a river! And yet the term "baptize" or "baptism" is rightly applied to both actions.

In fact, long before the New Testament period, the Greek word "baptize" and its variants already had several meanings. But all of those meanings were derived from the single, most basic notion of the word, which was "to dip, sink, or plunge into liquid." The word often was connected with the action of repeated plunging of cloth into water to wash it or dye it or plunging hands or eating utensils into water to clean them. The word also meant "to take a drink," but this, too, had a connotation with plunging, as in the action of dipping a cup or ladle into a vat of water or wine. Before the New Testament period, versions of the word *baptism* were also used more figuratively. One example connected sailors being plunged or immersed into the sea and was associated with the notion of "drowning" or "being shipwrecked." So by extension, the word occasionally meant "to perish."

Similar derivatives of baptism occasionally meant "to kill or be killed." Obviously, drowning in water suggests such an idea. But this meaning is also derived from the sense of "plunging" a sword into a person. This use of the word also plays on the other derived meaning, "to dye," as in to dye one's sword red with the blood of the victim or dye the clothes of the victim in the victim's own blood. Sophocles uses a word like baptism this way in one of his plays. It is easy, from these derived uses of the word, to see how St. Paul could later express the notion that baptism was a kind of death, as he does in his letter to the Romans when he writes that "we who were baptized into Christ Jesus were baptized into his death" (Rom 6:3).

Sources of the Word "Baptism"

A word connected with "baptism" is found in ancient Greek sources referring to pagan *religious* rites of bathing and washing. These included the Eleusinian rites that recalled the death and rising of Persephone, daughter of Demeter, the goddess of agriculture and fertility. The pagan cults of Bacchus, Isis, Mithras, and Serapis all included ritual immersions or washings described with the word "baptize."

Beyond the ancient Greco-Roman world, we find similar religious significance made of washings and immersions in ancient Egypt, Babylon, Persia, and India. Many of these pagan "baptisms" were connected to a similarly religious sense of new life or renewed life that resulted from the ritual bath. For example, in ancient Egypt, one need only think of the many depictions of *ankhs* ♀ being poured over the body of the dead pharaoh to awaken him to new life in the netherworld. The Greek historian Herodotus wrote that one who drowns, or is killed by a crocodile, in the sacred waters of the Nile River in Egypt, is "baptized" in those sacred waters. There were separate ancient Egyptian funeral rites reserved exclusively for a person who died in the Nile.

It is important to note that the use of the word *baptize* within the contexts of these pagan rites does not mean the word itself had an exclusive religious or sacred sense. While the use of "baptize" in these examples was used to mean a dip, plunge, or wash, the term did not describe the rite itself. Rather, the dipping, plunging, or washing was understood only as *part* of the rite. No one would have described one who had completed the pagan rites of Bacchus or Serapis, for example, as having been "baptized" into the group in the way that modern Christians refer to one who becomes a Christian by having been "baptized."

Forms of the word *baptism* occur about two dozen times in the Septuagint, the Greek translation of the Old Testament, which dates to the third century BC. About half of these occurrences have to do with explicit rituals. These are instances of a priest dipping hyssop into the blood of a sacrificed animal or the cleansing of a person (in a *mikvah*) or thing from ritual impurity (see Leviticus 14:48–53). The other instances of the word refer to such things as dipping bread in wine or vinegar or bathing or stepping into water. Greek forms of the word *baptism* were also used to describe the ritual washing of the hands by plunging hands into a basin of water for ritual cleansing. All cases of the word's use in the Old Testament—either in a sacred or banal context—have to do with dipping or plunging something into liquid.

How "Baptism" Is Used in the Gospels and in Acts of the Apostles

The word "baptize" and its variants (Baptist, baptism, washed, dipped, etc.) occur some 116 times in the New Testament. Thirty times the noun "baptism" is used specifically to mean the religious ritual of Christian initiation. However, there are five occasions in the New Testament where the word "baptize" is used in a secular way, simply to mean "dipping" (see Luke 16:24, John 13:26, Revelation 19:13) or "washing" (see Mark 7:4, Luke 11:38).

Most often in the gospels, the term is used to describe John the Baptist or in reference to what he was doing or saying, for example, the action of "being baptized by him in the Jordan River" (Mk 1:5; 9) or quoting John when he says that "the one who is coming. . . . He will baptize you with the holy Spirit and fire" (Mt 3:11). Sixteen of the times we find the term in the New Testament are used as the title for St. John *the Baptist*. While it sounds comical to say it, I think that in some sense the Greek phrase for "John the Baptist" would have been read or heard by a first century Greek speaker as "John the Plunger!" But I am quick to note that the word "plunger" most certainly did *not* connote, for that first century Greek speaker, what the word "plunger" now means for the twenty-first century-English speaker!

In Acts of the Apostles, a form of the verb baptize is found eighteen times, always referring to the Christian ritual of baptism, for example, Peter directing the throngs of Pentecost pilgrims to "Repent and be baptized, every one of you, in the name of Jesus Christ for the forgiveness of your sins; and you will receive the gift of the holy Spirit" (Acts 2:38). This suggests that within the primitive Christian communities, by the time of the writing of Acts in the late first century, the term exclusively referred to the initiation rite of baptism. One of the latest books of the New Testament, the First Letter of Peter, describes the saving, forgiving nature of baptism (see 1 Peter 3:18–22).

How "Baptism" Is Used in the Letters of St. Paul

Recall that though the Pauline letters are arranged after the gospels in the New Testament, they were actually written some decades before the gospels. In the letters of Paul, as in Acts, the words "baptize" and "baptism" are never used in the secular sense of dipping or washing but only in the cultic sense, referring to the Christian rite of baptism. And, it was Paul who infused the rite (and the term itself) with the rich, theological understanding that would become the basis for subsequent Christian teaching about the Sacrament of Baptism.

For example, Paul is the first to speak of baptism in terms of Christ's death (see Romans 6:3–5). He is the first to infuse the term (and the ritual) with the theology of dying and rising with Christ in the waters of baptism: "You were buried with him in baptism, in which you were also raised with him through faith in the power of God, who raised him from the dead" (Col 2:12). It is Paul who first used the image of the baptized being "clothed" in Christ (see Galatians 3:27). Early Christian baptism was generally understood in this Pauline way: being immersed/baptized in Christ (sometimes expressed as "in Christ's name") and thereby dying with him. St. Paul's theological understanding of the rite of baptism would become the normative theology of the sacrament.

What the New Testament Says about How Baptism Was Celebrated

What was the rite of baptism like in the early Church? Were new Christians "dipped" in water or was water "sprinkled" over their heads or both? Perhaps surprisingly, we're not exactly sure. We have many Christian sources from antiquity giving accounts of the ritual in a particular Christian community at a particular time. But there is no reason to believe that the ritual of baptism was uniform from place to place or age to age in the early Church. Many of these sources describe anointings both before and after the baptism. They describe the declaration of creedal formulas prior to baptism. Several sources mention that the hand of the baptizer—the bishop, priest, or deacon—was placed on the head of the person being baptized in order to push the person's head down into the water. Some sources note that the person is baptized in the nude and, after coming up out of the baptismal pool, is dressed again while prayers are offered to accompany the redressing of the baptized individual. So we can infer from these non-biblical sources that a large enough pool for immersion of the person was in place. Unfortunately, these non-biblical accounts do not give us a definitive answer to what was the "dipping" or "immersing" action conveyed by the use of the Greek word for baptism.

The New Testament itself is equally unclear on how exactly baptisms were celebrated during this period. For example, in Acts 10:47–48 Peter calls for the baptism of a Roman centurion Cornelius, his relatives, and close friends (see Acts 10:24). Where and how were these people—including, we presume, Cornelius's wife, children, relatives, slaves—baptized? There is no mention of a river or pool nearby. Perhaps a pool is to be understood within the context of the Roman villa of Cornelius, a prominent imperial authority figure. Or maybe, being in the coastal city of Caesarea Maritima, perhaps Cornelius's villa was a seaside villa with easy access to the sea. Acts of the Apostles does not provide these details. It may well be that the New Testament authors simply assumed that readers would understand the word *baptism* without need for further elaboration, that "baptize" means "to plunge," pure and simple.

The original pre-Christian, secular meanings of baptism and its associated terms—derived from the idea of sinking or plunging into water and also associated in some cases with dying and death—certainly provided Paul with some help and insight into Christ's saving action in the baptismal ritual that he used in developing his theology around baptism, which he included in his New Testament letters.

‹ 13 ›

Why Doesn't *Abba* Mean "Daddy"?

The two ideas that the word "abba"—the word Jesus uses to address God—is an expression of close intimacy, the kind of word a child uses for "father," and that Jesus' using this word to address God is unique, unheard of in the history of Judaism, are very widely accepted by Christians. But these claims are simply not true. Yet it is a notion that many scholars, as well as persons in the pew, hold to very tightly. It has been so oft repeated and popularized that most Catholics as well as many scholars simply take it for granted. However, scholarship simply does not support either the notion of intimacy or the idea that the use of the word to address God is unique to Jesus. In fact, the word does *not* connote intimacy and it is a word addressed to God that was *used frequently* within Jewish writings and prayers.

The person who promoted this mistaken idea was a great German biblical scholar, Joachim Jeremias (1900–1979). His wonderful academic career focused especially on the Judaism of Jesus' day. This interest pushed him into both rabbinic and linguistic studies to understand the theological thought-world of Jesus. Without a doubt, he understood both Hebrew and Aramaic better than most.

In 1958, Jeremias published an article in German in a scholarly, New Testament book. In that article, Jeremias first proposed two ideas. First, he wrote that the word *abba* was a word reserved only for a context of great intimacy, like that between a child and a father. Second, Jeremias claimed that the use of this very familial word to address God was unique to Jesus—unheard of in Judaism before Jesus used it. Jeremias would address these ideas again in a later book, *The Prayers of Jesus*, published in English in 1967. In this second book, Jeremias backs away a bit from suggesting that the word *abba* is derived from the babbling sound made by a child in the arms of his or her father. But he still asserts, "Indeed, the address means even more . . . Jesus' use of *Abba* expresses a special relationship with God."

So how could an expert of Jeremias's stature make such a mistake? Well the simple translation of this word is not as simple as you might think. In fact, it is a very complicated problem—a problem with many difficult aspects to it.

Origins of the Word "Abba"

The first challenge is simply figuring out what language the word "abba" comes from. The New Testament books are all written in Greek. In each of the three places this word is found in the New Testament (Mark 14:36, Romans 8:15, and Galatians 4:6) the word is transliterated, written with Greek letters, although it is not a Greek word. Both Mark and Paul have simply used Greek letters to transliterate the word into readable Greek. But this begs the question: From what language is this word?

It is either Aramaic or Hebrew. And this is the most important issue concerning the interpretation of this word. Since Jesus' mother tongue was Aramaic, it is most probably an Aramaic word, an Aramaic word that in the New Testament has been transliterated with Greek letters. Those letters are the equivalent in English of *a-b-b-a*. (Yes, pronounced like the name of the internationally popular Swedish music sensation ABBA of the '70s and '80s.) Hold that thought for a moment—that the word *abba* is an Aramaic word.

But abba could also be a Hebrew word. Hebrew and Aramaic are very similar languages. Both are Semitic languages, and both use the same alphabet. They are closely related to each other, somewhat the way French and Italian are similar. In fact, in today's modern Israel, young Hebrew-speaking children refer to their fathers as *abba*. So it is definitely true that in modern Hebrew this is a word that means "daddy" or "papa." And this is probably the source of Jeremias's first confusion about the word.

Between the ages of ten and eighteen, Joachim Jeremias lived in Jerusalem, where his father was the Provost of the Lutheran Church of the Redeemer. While there he doubtlessly frequently heard young Hebrew-speaking children calling to their fathers as *abba*.

However, when this meaning of abba is looked at through the eyes of ancient, biblical Hebrew, it looks very odd. The typical word in ancient, biblical Hebrew for father is not abba but *ab* (pronounced ahb, with the "a" sounding like the "a" in Bach). There was no final "a" at the end of the word in ancient, biblical Hebrew. So why do modern Hebrew-speaking children living in Israel today refer to their fathers as abba and not *ab*?

The answer is because the word is not Hebrew but Aramaic!

How the Aramaic Word "Abba" Came to Be Used in the Bible and in Modern Hebrew

Since the fifth century BC, the people living in the land of Israel spoke Aramaic, not Hebrew. Aramaic was the language used by Persia for the administration of the conquered territories it gained when it swept through the region in the mid-fifth century BC. It is probable that through the centuries, in and through the time of Jesus, that the Aramaic word *abba* endured among the Jewish population, remaining in use—passed from parent to child—through the period in which Aramaic was the language of the region until Hebrew was reinvented into the form of modern Hebrew that is spoken in Israel today.

By way of example, think of the many "foreign" words that have become part of and endured in American English vocabulary: the German *Kindergarten* or the Italian *bravo* or the French *hors d'oeuvre*, etc. So common have these words become in American life that most of us think of them as English words. The word *abba* likewise passed from its home in the Aramaic language spoken in Israel during Jesus' time into modern Hebrew, spoken in today's Israel.

So, now let's look at the word *abba* as it most probably is: an Aramaic word. And as an Aramaic word, it looks quite normal. By that I mean that the word for "father" in Aramaic is, just like in Hebrew, *ab*. But in Aramaic, unlike Hebrew, the definite article—the word "the" in English—does not come *before* the noun, but *after* the noun, attached to the end. And what is the definite article, the word for "the" in Aramaic? It is *a*, pronounced as *aaah* (like "Aaah, that beer tastes great!"). And how would one write the Aramaic words "the father" transliterated in Greek letters? They would be written as *abba*, with the definite article *a* coming after the noun, *ab*.

This all seems very complex, but it's really much simpler than we think. Let's forget about ancient grammar and vocabulary for a moment and see how the writers of the New Testament themselves understood and wrote the word. In each of the three places where this Aramaic word (written in Greek letters) is found in the Gospel of Mark and in Paul's letters, we find that the authors *themselves* have conveniently translated the Aramaic word into Greek for their readers. And how do they translate it into Greek? They translate it as *ho pater* (*ο ρατηρ*). *Pater* means "father" and *ho* means "the" in Greek, so the translation would be "abba," "the father." This is hardly the baby talk of a child to its father! No, on the contrary, adding the article "the" to the word in the Aramaic-speaking culture made it more of a formal address by Jesus to his Father, almost like a title. It is what a grammarian would call the "vocative use," the form of a noun used for direct address of a person.

And as much as Joachim Jeremias and other scholars have learned about the ancient languages of the Bible, I'm sure that Paul and the author of Mark's gospel were far more familiar with their usage of *abba* than we modern "experts." Certainly neither Paul nor Mark translate *abba* as anything like "daddy" or "papa." That is indisputably clear.

But if *abba* was meant to communicate Jesus' familiar, child-like relationship with his Father, Paul and the author of Mark could have translated it that way. There were perfectly good Greek words in use within Greek at that time and in that part of the world that meant "papa" or "daddy." There were a variety of such words for "daddy" the writers could have chosen from in ancient Greek: *patridion, papas, pappas, pappias*, or *pappidion*. In fact, two ancient-Greek writers who are just about contemporary with the writing of the New Testament, Cornutus and Epicurus, both use the word *papas* for "daddy" in their writings. So if Paul or Mark had wanted to translate *Abba* as "papa" or "daddy," they certainly could have done so. But they didn't; they translated the phrase each time into Greek as more formally "the father."

The Uniqueness of Jesus' Addressing God as Father

Now, on to the other mistaken notion of Joachim Jeremias: that Jesus' address of God in prayer as "Father" was unknown and unheard of until Jesus said it. First, let us be clear: what Jeremias *intended* was that the term *abba* was a term of intimacy and that it was Jesus' *intimate usage* of addressing God that was unique to Jesus, not that addressing God as Father was unique. Still, over time the idea that simply addressing God as Father was peculiar or unique to Jesus grew and spread since Jeremias had published his work. It is not unusual still today to hear and read that addressing God as Father was unheard of until Jesus did so. But this, too, is completely untrue.

Ancient peoples—both Jews and Gentiles—have frequently addressed God as "father" for centuries. In fact, addressing the Greek god Zeus as father was so common that the Greek phrase *Zeus, pater* ("father Zeus") eventually became corrupted as the Roman name for the god, Jupiter. The Greek address of *Zeus pater* (pronounced *dzheu-pater*) was repeated so often that it eventually slurred together into *dzheus-pater*, then *dzeus-piter*, until it eventually became Jupiter, the Latin name for Zeus.

Closer to the world of ancient Israel, we find God called "father" in several places throughout the Old Testament. God is addressed as father in Deuteronomy (32:6), Jeremiah (3:4, 31:9), Isaiah (63:16), and in later Old Testament works such as Tobit (13:4), Wisdom (14:3), and Sirach (4:10; 23:1, 4; 51:10). The name father is even found in two manuscripts of a Jewish psalm prayer found among the Dead Sea Scrolls (not included in modern Bibles).

Furthermore, many ancient Jewish prayers address God as "father," particularly in a prayer known by the title *Abinu Malkenu* ("Our Father, Our King") that is still recited by Jews today. In fact, a version of this prayer set to music was recently recorded by Barbra Streisand.

Jesus prayed like most other Jews of his time. That Jesus would have learned to pray like his Jewish contemporaries only makes sense (see chapter 15, "What Are the Origins of the Lord's Prayer?"). And we now know that Jesus' fellow Jews prayed to God, addressing him as Father as a matter of normal course. But many of us want to find Jesus unique in each and every aspect of his life and ministry and thus remove him from the Jewish, cultural world in which God chose to incarnate him. That exaggerated desire to make Jesus unique, to divorce him from his religious and historical milieu, can actually interfere with our understanding of just who Jesus is, what he seeks to teach us, and how his own followers understood him.

Scholars make mistakes. New data becomes available. Someone digging a new subway in Jerusalem or Rome turns up inscriptions in stone, hitherto unknown. An ancient papyrus is coughed up by the sands of Egypt. Ancient manuscripts are found in a cave by the Dead Sea. Any number of factors contribute to ongoing biblical scholarship that causes foregone conclusions to change and previously popular theories to be abandoned. So let's not heap blame on Dr. Jeremias! But repeating errors over and over again do not make them true. The goal of Catholic biblical scholarship is to account for the data that we have and, when necessary, as when new data comes to light, to correct earlier misinterpretations and conclusions.

‹ 14 ›

What Is the Kingdom of God *Really* Like?

The kingdom of God (also called the kingdom of heaven; Jesus uses both versions interchangeably) is a central theme of Jesus' preaching. You could argue that Jesus' instruction about God's kingdom is the whole point of his preaching! Further, you could say that a major purpose of Jesus becoming human was to announce, initiate, and invite us into the kingdom of God. This begs the questions: "What is the kingdom of God?" and "What is the kingdom of God *really* like?" Answering these questions takes some thought. Jesus rarely offers straightforward answers. He more often uses analogies, parables, and comparisons (e.g., "the kingdom of God is like . . .") to help us come up with answers. There are several "kingdom of God" references in the gospels that allow a varied and interesting look into what the kingdom of God is really like. I am going to focus on one perspective in particular.

When I began to study the comments Jesus makes about the kingdom of God, I noticed something that I found very interesting and puzzling. When Jesus teaches with parables about the kingdom of God, some things are visible and some things are invisible to the characters in his parables. This element is present in many of Jesus' statements about the kingdom, and it actually becomes a kind of lens through which you can begin to derive much more meaning from Jesus' teaching about the kingdom.

Let me explain. When I lived in Rome, I was often surrounded by native Roma kids—especially at crowded tourist sites like the Trevi fountain or the Coliseum—who were trying to pick my pocket! One kid used a special tactic. He printed in English on a large piece of cardboard a plea that said something like "I'm Hungry!" The kid came really close to me and held the placard right under my chin, against my throat. At first I thought he did that so I could more easily read his message. But in fact, this piece of cardboard was shielding my field of vision, restricting my sight to only what was above the cardboard sign while making invisible all that was going on beneath the piece of cardboard. And what was going on beneath the cardboard was that my pockets were being picked! (Or at least the boy and his partners were trying to pick my pockets.) Keep this image of a "barrier of invisibility" in mind as we talk about some of the parables Jesus uses to teach us about the kingdom of God.

There are some similarities to the barrier of invisibility provided by the Roma kid's cardboard placard and what Jesus describes in his parables about the kingdom of God. Let's look at a few examples.

The Parables and Barriers of Invisibility

Take the parable of the lost coin (Lk 15:8–10): the woman with the ten silver coins has lost one of them and sweeps the whole house in order to find it. Lo and behold, she finds her lost coin! But was the coin really lost? Or, was it just not visible to her? In fact, the "lost" coin was never out of her possession. It was in her house the whole time. I think this parable is not only about the joy of finding something that was lost but also about discovering that the thing she was looking for was there all along—she just couldn't see it. There was a kind of barrier of invisibility that prevented her from finding it.

Or, think of the short parable of the yeast (Mt 13:33, Lk 13:20–21): "The kingdom of heaven is like yeast that a woman took and mixed with three measures of wheat flour until the whole batch was leavened." Have you ever baked bread? If so, do you recall the first time you tried it? I was an on-and-off cook in our friary for several years and tried to learn how to bake bread. I recall mixing what was really a very simple recipe—basically flour, salt, yeast, and water. The recipe told me to mix all the ingredients and then leave it in a warm spot for an hour or two and then return to remix and knead the dough again. So I left the mixture in a small stainless steel bowl near the radiator in the kitchen, only to return to find that it had grown to what I called "the dough that ate Cleveland!" I was shocked to find that the dough had expanded beyond the top of the small bowl and was flopping in bits onto the floor! The action of the yeast that happened while I was gone was not only unknown to me but also *invisible* to me. Who knew that a little envelope of yeast could do *that* to a little bit of flour and water?

Jesus also compares the kingdom of heaven to a mustard seed in Matthew 13:31–32. Have you ever seen a mustard seed? They really are small. Wikipedia says they're between .039 and .079 inches in diameter. That's small! Now, how could anyone know just looking at that tiny thing that inside of it, under the right conditions and over time, from that miniscule seed would grow a large tree? The elements of that large tree are basically "in there," but such potential is invisible to us as we look at the tiny seed. But if you put that tiny thing in the right soil, add the right amount of sunlight and water, and return in a few years, you'd be shocked to find that what had been invisible to you in that tiny speck had the amazing potential to become a tree.

Then there is a string of short parables in Matthew 13:44–50. In the first of these, Jesus says the kingdom of heaven is like a treasure buried in a field. That treasure had been buried there for who knows how long, invisible, until suddenly a man finds it and sells all that he has in order to get enough money to buy the field and the treasure that came with it. It was there all along, but no one could see it. Next is a short parable about a "pearl of great price." The merchant, Jesus says, has been searching for fine pearls, and finally he finds one. He too goes out to raise the capital he needs to buy this valuable pearl that was once out of sight, beyond his reach, but now is right before his eyes.

Similarly, Jesus says "the kingdom of heaven is like a net thrown into the sea, which collects fish of every kind" (Mt 13:47). Fishing is a perfect example of what I'm talking about. Quite literally, the surface of the water is a barrier to visibility. In most fishing waters you cannot, without the help of modern technical devices, see below the water's surface. You cannot see where the fish are. Imagine a young child fishing for the first time. When she feels the tug of her line, she knows something is going on. And, then, what a surprise when she reels in her line! Who could really have believed there were fish down there? The fish didn't suddenly appear when she dropped her line into the water. The fish were always there below the boat. She just couldn't see them. It's not until she pulled up her line that she realized there were fish under the surface of the water. The surprise is even more immense in the way that Jesus describes fishing: a large net captures "fish of every kind."

Let me share one more example. The parable of the ten virgins (or handmaids) in Matthew 25:1–13 also has this same theme of invisibility. The ten young women are awaiting the groom's arrival. They don't know when he will arrive. They know he is on his way, but they can't see him. He's taking longer than they thought, and five of the bridesmaids are running out of oil. If any of these five had thought about the eventual arrival of the bridegroom, as the other five apparently had, you can imagine them getting nervous about their burning up all this oil and knowing they were really going to need it when the man arrived. It'd be like driving a car without an accurate gas gauge!

Well, sure enough, the bridegroom shows up and becomes visible to them, and they realize they're out of oil for their lamps. They also realize that while they were burning their oil in the lamps, playing cards or dice or whatever, all that time the bridegroom was approaching; he was on his way. They just couldn't see him traveling toward them. Maybe at least one of them thought, "Geez, all this time while we were playing cards and wasting time, the groom *was* headed our way. If only I'd known."

There are several more examples of this theme of invisibility in Jesus' parables about the kingdom. You can also apply my principal to the famous parable of the prodigal (lost) son in Luke 15:11–32. While the prodigal son was yet a long way off, Jesus says, his father watched for him, but the runaway son never knew it. Jesus suggests this by saying "while he was still a long way off . . ." the father saw his son returning. The son didn't know how expected or anticipated his return would be. He didn't know his father had continued lovingly to look for him. In fact, the son, unable to see his father looking out his window for him (perhaps daily), feared he would not be welcomed when he returned. How many times does Jesus allude to this kind of thing? A lot! Jesus makes over fifty references to planting in the gospels. He talks about fishing more than forty times. And both of these common activities in Jesus' world literally contain this notion of invisibility. But more importantly, they have within them this same realization of a barrier to visibility.

The Kingdom of God Is Like a Surprise Gift!

There is always more to the story! When you read the scriptures and, in this particular case, the kingdom of God parables, and look for something that is at first glance hidden or invisible but right there lurking below the surface, you will be rewarded. A great deal of scripture scholarship and study involves such deep prayer and reflection.

Perhaps this personal story about my family and a gift I received will better help you understand this lesson. I believe that my two grandmothers never really got along very well. My mother's mother, Mame Devlin, strove to be as "lace-curtain Irish" as she could be, always very much aware of what the neighbors thought and how she and her four daughters appeared in public. I can remember how often my grandmother would chide my mother for not wearing gloves when she left the house. (With five children to care for, I'm quite sure that wearing or even *having* white gloves was *not* near the top of my mother's concerns!) My father's mother, Nancy Kilcullen Burton, widowed during the Great Depression and left to care for not only her own six children but also two of her nephews, had no airs about her whatsoever. If she had ever been described as "shanty Irish" by anyone, I doubt she'd have been offended. She would probably have considered it nothing but the simple truth. For this and for reasons I'm sure I'll never know, these two widows, though tied together by my parents' wedding and shared grandchildren, simply never liked each other very much. Similarly, the other relatives on both sides of my family never mingled much either.

So, ten years after my parents both had died and about nine months before my ordination, it seemed odd to me that my cousin Nancy Kay (on my father's side) called me and asked for the phone number of my Aunt Kate (on my mother's side). I gave Nancy Kay the number, but the request puzzled me. "What in the world does Nancy Kay want to talk to my Aunt Kate about?" I thought. But as my final semester in seminary wore on and preparations for ordination began, I simply forgot about Nancy Kay's phone call.

But then, on the day of my ordination, my cousin Nancy Kay approached me at the reception with a large package, beautifully wrapped and tied with a bow. It was big and heavy, and I couldn't imagine what was in it. When I opened it later, I discovered that it was a large photo album filled with photographs of my mother and father from all stages of their lives from childhood to adulthood. There were photos I had never seen before. And then it hit me: "Oh, *this* is why Nancy Kay wanted to talk to my Aunt Kate! She needed to get photos of my mom as a girl."

But then I had an even more impactful realization. Nancy Kay had called me *nine months* before my ordination. That meant that for almost a year, my cousin Nancy Kay was collecting, arranging, and pasting all these photos of my father, her "Uncle Jim," and my mother, her "Aunt Anne." For nine months while I was busy with school and all the stuff graduating students do, and while I was getting the ordination planned and prepared for, for all that time, invisible to me, my cousin was doing this great, touching act of kindness for me. And she was doing it with the help of my Aunt Kate and others on both sides of the family, some of whom had not been in contact for years. All of these loving actions over the course of nine months were hidden from me until the very moment I opened the package. Then, what had been invisible to me suddenly became clear. I could see and feel the surprising goodness that had been undertaken on my behalf.

The realization that someone had been dedicating time and talent to *create* this gift both tells a story of affection and affords the sudden realization that something for my benefit had been ongoing at a time when I was unaware of it. Isn't this also the impact of a surprise party? After the initial shock of a roomful of people screaming "Happy Birthday!" and scaring you out of your wits comes the dawning realization of how hard and for how long so many of your friends had been working to put this party together, all without you knowing about it.

I suspect that some will think that I'm reading too much into this idea of a barrier to visibility being in many of Jesus' descriptions of the kingdom of God. This is understandable since so many of these references of Jesus are oblique, implicit, or suggested rather than explicit and clear. Certainly, Jesus' words and actions are a witness to the *visibility* of God's kingdom. The kingdom of God was made visible in his miraculous cures. The kingdom of God was made visible by his acts of compassion for the people most hated in his society. But what about today? How is the kingdom of God made visible now?

When we follow Jesus' instruction to "go and do likewise" in imitation of the Good Samaritan, we become agents for breaking that barrier of visibility and bringing God's kingdom into the light of this world. When we do this kind of kingdom activity— heal the sick, care for widows and children, feed the hungry, visit the imprisoned, and more—we act like Jesus and make God's kingdom surprisingly visible to others.

An important corollary of this is that when our kindness makes the kingdom visible to someone, what is his or her reaction? I think of the many times I had to drive on this large, busy, and fast urban stretch of Interstate 90/94 in Chicago called the Dan Ryan. It was often almost impossible to get onto that expressway from the entrance ramps because everyone was so hurried, driving so fast to get where *they* were going that it was rare that anyone would let me in from an approaching lane. But on that rare occasion when someone did let me in front of them, I'd be so surprised by that act of kindness that the next time I was the driver with the opportunity to let someone in front of *me*, I'd think of that act of kindness shown to me and be moved to pass on that kindness to another person. And I'd let them onto the Dan Ryan!

When God's kingdom is suddenly made visible to me by some act of kindness, even while harried on a busy highway, my reaction to that sudden awareness is to act kindly to someone else and perhaps make the kingdom visible to that person. Thus awareness of the ever-present kingdom can spread. The more acts of kindness that we do, the clearer it will be to people that the kingdom of God is still present and churning, straining to become visible, like the sprig of a young plant that struggles to push through the dark soil into the life-giving sunlight. St. Paul referred to the process of journeying to Christ and seeking heavenly perfection as *epektasis*—an unending straining forward: "[F]orgetting what lies behind but straining forward to what lies ahead, I continue my pursuit toward the goal, the prize of God's upward calling, in Christ Jesus" (Phil 3:13). Just so, the kingdom struggles and strains to break into our world, struggles to be made visible. And thus we become not only witnesses but agents for the in-breaking of the kingdom in our world. Each act of loving kindness, each attempt to live as Jesus taught us, shows us and others that the kingdom of God is among us, running quietly in his love-filled creation, just beneath the surface of our consciousness.

≺ 15 ≻

What Are the Origins of the Lord's Prayer?

We are all familiar with the Lord's Prayer, the Our Father. It is a prayer many of us pray daily and often several times a day. Catholics pray a version that is a little shorter than the form of the prayer used in the Protestant traditions. There is evidence that Christians have been praying this prayer during the Eucharist from the earliest times. Ask any priest who has witnessed a marriage between a Roman Catholic and a Jew and he'll probably tell you that the one prayer that he and the rabbi agree that both the Jews and the Christians can pray together is the Our Father.

In fact, the prayer is so well known by so many of us that we often recite it almost automatically and without giving it any real thought. And yet the Our Father has a fascinating, theologically rich history. It is a prayer found in the gospels of Matthew (6:9–13) and Luke (11:2–4) with several phrases of the prayer also found in two places in the Gospel of Mark (11:25, 14:38). One of the most exciting aspects of the prayer is in fact its antiquity. This prayer has been prayed by Christians since the time of Jesus.

Akin to issues about Jesus' address of God as Father *abba* (treated in chapter 13), similar issues have arisen from studying the biblical texts about just how unique this prayer actually was to Jesus. It is and has been a tradition for millennia that the Our Father was first composed by Jesus and taught to his followers, making it a distinctive prayer for them. However, there is a good deal of evidence that the prayer is really part of a Jewish prayer and that Jesus probably learned this Jewish prayer from his parents.

I want to be clear. I think it is indisputable that Jesus prayed the Our Father and recommended it to his followers, much as described in both Matthew's and Luke's accounts. The point of contention is the source or sources for this prayer. The Lord's Prayer looks very much like an ancient Jewish prayer, an abbreviated form of the *amidah*, a prayer prayed by Jews three times a day. The *amidah* also is known as the "Eighteen Benedictions" and was in existence well before Jesus was born. The *amidah* is both a private prayer (recited by Jews silently every day) and, in other forms, is part of the public synagogue services. There are various forms of the prayer used at different times and occasions (weekdays, the Sabbath, festivals) and in different geographical locations.

We must always keep in mind that Jesus was a Jew who lived in Palestine in the early part of the first century AD. Therefore, it is reasonable to think that, as in many aspects of Jesus' thought and actions, he also thought and behaved and prayed as a first-century Jew. Noted biblical scholar James Charlesworth also reminds us that, as Jews, Jesus and his followers "inherited the prayers developed by common folk, and structured the day through the statutory public prayers, recited in the morning, afternoon and evening."[1]

Given this premise and background, let's take a look at the origins of the Lord's Prayer and break open in more detail some of the meaning of its petitions.

Tracing the Origins of the Lord's Prayer

Let's start backward, beginning with the earliest Christian source *outside* the gospels of Matthew and Luke and work back in time to see if we can discern a trail of historical evidence for roots of the Lord's Prayer.

The prayer appears outside the New Testament in an ancient Christian text called the *Didache*. The *Didache* is a manual or primitive catechism that was used by early Christians for evangelizing Gentiles. It claims it is a compilation of the teachings of the apostles. The *Didache* is a composite document, made up of parts that come from older sources. Its final form appears to have come together at least by AD 150, but most scholars speculate that parts of it are probably older. Many date the main text to the late first century.

This early Christian instruction manual was written by Jewish followers of Jesus to help in the conversion of Gentiles. The *Didache* states rules for praying the Lord's Prayer—"Pray thus three times a day" (VIII, 3)—which was consistent with the Jewish practice of praying the *amidah* three times a day. This suggests that at least early Jewish Christians thought the Lord's Prayer should be prayed as often and at the same times as the *amidah*.

Moving further back in time to Jewish sources, it's important to remember that dating these texts of the *amidah* is very difficult. Jewish tradition holds that the *amidah* was promulgated by the Great Assembly or the Great Synagogue (the *beit din*). This was an assembly of religious leaders that ruled Judaism from the beginning of the second Temple period, circa 530 BC until the Maccabean period in the second century BC. If this tradition is true, then the prayer could be dated as early as the sixth century BC. However, the earliest history of the Great Synagogue is very much disputed by historians.

Another challenge to accurately dating the *amidah* is that the Talmud (the central text for religious law and theology) specifically states that the benedictions of the *amidah* were *not* to be written down (*Tosef, Shab* 13:4). This explains why finding the text of the prayer on ancient papyrus or parchment has proved to be *almost* impossible. However, some texts have survived. Eight different versions of the *amidah* are cited in the Talmud, which gives instructions on how to pray it. In one citation, the Talmud tells us that the prayer should not be recited as one would read a letter, but the person praying the *amidah* should say something new in the daily recitation of the prayer.

It seems there was no effort by Jewish leadership to codify the prayer until the late first century AD, implying that it is much older than the time of its final codification. Before it was formalized, the prayer form of the *amidah* was very malleable, consistent with the instructions of the Talmud. Elements could also be arranged in a different sequence, or some elements could simply be dropped. It was not to be recited from memory nor read from a written text. In the Jewish tradition, it was to be prayed spontaneously, from the heart.

Third-century Christian writers Tertullian and Origen both believed that the Lord's Prayer similarly ought *not* be recited by rote but that the prayer should only suggest an outline or a form for prayer. Cyprian, another ancient Christian writer, said that all Christian prayer ought to be modeled on the Lord's Prayer and that the priest ought to pray the prayer spontaneously in the presence of a congregation. This all sounds very much like the way ancient Jews understood the praying of the *amidah*.

When considering whether Jesus composed the Our Father and its various petitions, it is important to show evidence for *when* the words of this prayer were first being prayed. If there is no evidence for the words of the Lord's Prayer being prayed prior to Jesus, then the argument that Jesus composed the prayer is strengthened. If, however, there is evidence to support that the prayer was being prayed by Jews before Jesus, that would support the argument that it was a prayer already in circulation *before* the time of Jesus.

Parts of the *Amidah* Compared to the Lord's Prayer

Given this understanding of Jewish prayer and even early Christian instructions about the Lord's Prayer, rather than looking for the prayer as we know it today in ancient sources, let's look at parts of the *amidah* and compare these individual parts to elements in the Lord's Prayer as well as to Old Testament and other Jewish sources. There are six parts of the *amidah* that can be isolated and their history traced:

1. The address of God as Father
2. The blessing of God's name
3. Asking for the coming of God's kingdom
4. The petition for daily bread
5. The request for conditional forgiveness of sin
6. Begging for deliverance from trial and temptation

1. The Address of God as Father ("Our Father")

Without repeating in detail the information on this topic from chapter 13, suffice to say here that praying to God as "our Father" was found throughout Judaism and even in ancient paganism. Some of the places where God is addressed this way in the Old Testament are Deuteronomy 32:6; Malachi 2:10; Psalms 68:6, 89:27, 103:13; Jeremiah 3:4, 31:9; and several other places (e.g., Tobit, Wisdom, and Sirach). There is also the important discovery from the Dead Sea Scrolls, mentioned earlier, which contain an extra-biblical psalm and one other Jewish prayer, both of which address God as "Father."

As previously mentioned, God is addressed as Father in the Jewish prayer, the *Abinu Malkenu*, the name of which is taken from the first line of the prayer: "Our Father, Our King." This phrase is attested by Rabbi Akiba, who lived between AD 50 and 135. We find this same address in Jewish prayers being prayed at the same time outside the land of Israel.

2. The Blessing of God's Name ("Hallowed Be Thy Name")

Asking that God or God's name be "hallowed" or "blessed" was extremely common in the prayers of ancient Judaism. First Chronicles quotes King David blessing the Lord in sight of the whole assembly (29:10). A vision was relayed to Daniel in a dream and he offered this blessing: "Blessed be the name of God forever and ever, for wisdom and power are his" (Dn 2:20).

Almost all forms of the prayer prayed at the end of a synagogue service called the *Kaddish* contain blessings for God's name. A particular form of the *Kaddish* is also prayed by mourners during funeral rites for the deceased. (This prayer also includes another portion that is very similar to a phrase in the Lord's Prayer; see pages 147–48.) It should be noted that the phrase "blessed be he" after an address or reference to God is so common in Jewish tradition that its occurrences are too numerous to count.

3. Asking for the Coming of God's Kingdom ("Thy Kingdom Come")

Praying for the coming of God's kingdom is part of a wider prayer tradition in Judaism that longs for the restoration of the Temple and of the holy city of Jerusalem. The loss of the holy city and Temple represents an ancient hurt in Judaism that goes back to the threatening Assyrian onslaught in the eighth century BC and the actual destruction of the Temple and city by the Babylonians in the sixth century BC. The final destruction of King Herod's rebuilt Temple by the Romans took place during New Testament times in AD 70. The longing for this sacred building and its environs continues today in the reverence we see in modern Jews for the Western (or Wailing) Wall—*ha Kotel*—the only remaining piece of the ancient Temple complex. The future restoration of the Temple has always been tied in Jewish consciousness with the longed-for restoration of God's kingdom.

Praying for God's kingdom has been scattered throughout Jewish prayer for millennia. We see it in the Bible itself in several texts; for example: "Treat Zion kindly according to your good will; build up the walls of Jerusalem" (Ps 51:20) and "Afterward all of them will return from their captivity, and they will rebuild Jerusalem with due honor" (Tb 14:5). In the non-biblical book of Second Baruch, which dates from circa AD 70 and possibly earlier, we find a long prayer from Baruch asking for God's establishment of his long-awaited kingdom (2 Baruch 21:19–26).

Praying for the coming of God's kingdom is also found in old versions of the *amidah*. For example, from fourteenth benediction of the current Ashkenazi version of the *amidah* we find this form of the petition: "Return in mercy to Jerusalem, your City. Dwell in it, as you have promised. Rebuild it soon and in our days. . . . And speedily set up in it the throne of David."

Certainly, there is clear evidence that prayers for the coming of God's kingdom had been part of Jewish prayer at the time of

Jesus, were present long before the time of Jesus, and are still in use today.

4. The Petition for Daily Bread ("Give Us This Day Our Daily Bread")

In discussing this petition for "daily bread," I'd like to first share some additional reflections about the word "daily." The English word "daily" is an attempt to translate the Greek word *epiousion*. What is fascinating about this small word and worthy of extra discussion is that no one is sure just what it means!

In linguistic circles the word "daily" in Greek literature is classified as a *hapax legomenon*. This means it is a word that occurs only once within a particular body of literature or within the record of all the literature of a language. And that is the case with this word. The Greek word for daily, *epiousion*, is unknown in *all* of Greek literature, except as it occurs in the two versions of the Lord's Prayer found in Matthew and Luke.

"So what?" you may be thinking. But if you give it a little more thought, you'll see that if a word occurs in only one text, in one literary context only, then you cannot really define it. We learn the full meaning of a word by seeing it or using it within several different contexts and by contrasting and comparing its use. Take the word "bore" for example. We might say, "The movie was a real bore." Or, "The student really bore down on his studies to prepare for the final exam." And, "The miner had to bore deep holes into the rock." (See my earlier example of the various uses of the word "hit" on page 81.) It is reading this word within different, albeit brief but varied, contexts that helps us to understand the variety of the word's meanings and to hone in on its nuances. The word *epiousion* is a word with *no* variety of contexts, *no* variety of perspectives to clarify its meaning. So how do we know what it means?

Actually, we don't and neither did ancient biblical scholars. So where does our translation "daily" come from? One interesting place to look is in the work of St. Jerome.

St. Jerome translated the Bible from Hebrew and Greek into Latin, at the request of Pope Damasus, in the early fifth century. Strangely, Jerome used three Latin words—quite different Latin words at that—to translate this *single* Greek word. In Matthew, Jerome *invented* a Latin word for *epiousion*: *supersubstantialem* which means "supersubstantial." Where the Greek word occurs in Luke's version of the prayer, Jerome chose a different Latin word: *quotidianus* meaning "daily." And then, in a commentary on the Gospel of Matthew, Jerome used yet another Latin word for *epiousion*: *crastinum*, which means "tomorrow's." And Jerome is not alone in the confusion of ancient scholars as to just what the word meant. Origen, a native Greek speaker and ancient biblical scholar, also confesses that he simply did not know this Greek word. He said he believed that *epiousion* was a word made up in Greek in an attempt to translate Jesus' original Aramaic word. He believed that those who translated Jesus' words from Aramaic to Greek simply did not know how to translate it.

Even before St. Jerome's translation of the Bible, there was confusion over how to translate *epiousion* in the Our Father. In some Latin translations, older than St. Jerome's work, the word is translated to mean "daily." A very ancient Syriac version translates the word as "continuous." Another Syriac manuscript uses "necessary" to convey the meaning of *epiousion*. One Egyptian version uses "coming." Two other Egyptian manuscripts translate the word as "tomorrow's." As my students would say: "Whaaaaat?" Clearly there is a problem here.

If you analyze the Greek word, you can see the reason for all the confusion. Bear with me as I try to break the word apart, to drill down on it a bit in order to at least get close to some probabilities for capturing the sense of this word.

The word is composed of two distinct parts, *epi*—a Greek preposition that usually means "upon" or "on"—and *ousion*—a word that could be a form of two different Greek verbs. When *epi* is affixed to one form of the verb it would mean "come upon," and when *epi* is affixed to the other form of the verb it would mean "be at" or "be on." Other ancient scholars thought that *ousion* was not a form of a verb at all but a noun, meaning "one's own" or "one's property" or "one's due." If that is true, then the word *epiousion* would mean something like "one's own" or "what is owed to someone." Not very helpful, right?

Okay, let's take another whack at it from a more practical approach. Is the word *epiousion* really a *hapax legomenon*? That is, has the word, or a word similar to it, ever been found elsewhere? Well, there are tantalizing hints that this word *might* not be a *hapax legomenon* and might have been used outside the New Testament. A very similar word is found in Plato's writings, specifically in his book *Crito*, and in one place Plato uses a word like this word to modify "day" so that it means "this day" or "today" and "this night." But in another place where Plato uses the same word—again to modify "night"—it means "coming" as in the phrase, "the coming night."

In 1925, a scholar reported that there was a record, dating to 1889, of a fragment of a papyrus that had *epiousion* on it. That fragment was apparently part of a list of provisions for a man's household, a kind of grocery list. This suggests that *epiousion* referred to a "daily ration" of some foodstuff, like a day's worth of chickpeas or lentils. Unfortunately this papyrus fragment has been lost. Another tantalizing bit is that in 1927, a scholar reported on an inscription on a wall in Pompeii that appeared to include the word *epiousion*. But sadly, the scholar said that upon revisiting the writing later, the inscription had "succumbed to the weather." As you can see, this investigation of one simple word has all the marks of an episode of a TV detective series.

When I step way back from the word in the gospels of Matthew and Luke and look at the Lord's Prayer within the much larger context of Jesus' teachings, I think, and this is only my opinion, that the word *epiousion* does mean "daily" but daily in the sense of "just for today, the 'ration' of bread that I need only for today." This would be consistent with so much of Jesus' teaching that urges us not to store up treasures. It would make the prayer sound like Jesus' parable criticizing the foolish man who built storehouses for all his riches (Lk 12:20–21) or like Jesus telling us to rely on God for what we need and not to worry about what we are to eat or what we are to wear (Mt 6:25–31; Lk 12:22). In so many places, Jesus tries to find ways to explain to us that we must trust that God loves us and that in his love, God will provide for all our needs. So I think *epiousion does* mean "daily" but only in the sense of "just for today" or "just enough for the day that is coming," reminding us to put a check on our greed, our need for security, and to truly *trust* God's love for us.

When we translate *epiousion* to mean a kind of daily wage or daily ration of bread ("just enough bread for today"), then we *do* find this specific petition in Jewish prayer before the time of Christ. Remember that dating Jewish prayers in general and specific portions of Jewish prayers is very difficult. However, I think it is well established that given the Jewish understanding that prayer was to be spontaneous, we can assume that such prayers are far older than the later written versions of them found in the historical record. For example, a prayer for just the food that is needed is Proverbs 30:8: "Put falsehood and lying far from me, give me neither poverty nor riches; provide me only with the food I need."

Similarly, this kind of petition is found in the *amidah* from the Tannaitic period of the first century AD. The thirteenth benediction reads: "Give us good pay for those who do Thy will . . ." In most versions of the *amidah*, the prayer for food is usually found in the ninth benediction, a benediction frequently taken out of the context of the larger prayer and used by Jews as a prayer before meals.

5. The Request for Conditonal Forgiveness of Sin ("And Forgive Us Our Trespasses, as We Forgive Those Who Trespass against Us")

The Ashkenazi version of the *amidah* states: "Forgive us, our Father, for we have sinned. Pardon us, our King, for we have transgressed." This is remarkably similar to the corresponding element of the Lord's Prayer. The notion that the forgiveness of our sins by God depends on our forgiveness of those who sin against us is also found in the Old Testament: "Forgive your neighbor the wrong done to you; then when you pray, your own sins will be forgiven" (Sir 28:2).

There are several ancient rabbinic statements concerning the conditional nature of God's forgiveness. Most of them state that if you have mercy on others then God will have mercy on you. One specific rabbinic statement reads: "He who is merciful to others, mercy is shown to him by heaven, while he who is not merciful to others, mercy is not shown to him by heaven."[2]

6. Begging for Deliverance from Trial and Temptation ("And Lead Us Not into Temptation, but Deliver Us from Evil")

This particular petition of the Lord's Prayer is the one that stirred controversy when Pope Francis suggested that the phrase "lead us not into temptation" has been mistranslated. The pope suggested that a better translation from the Greek to English would be something like "Do not let us fall into temptation." The pope's reasoning was clear and appropriate. In fact, this idea of deliverance from temptation is found in many ancient sources. In the

Old Testament, we find this idea of asking God's protection from evil in several places, including the Psalms: "You will protect them and those will rejoice in you who love your name" (5:12). God is called a shield, a rock, a refuge, and a deliverer. Also, the book of Sirach states: "No evil can harm the one who fears the Lord; through trials, again and again he is there" (33:1).

There are other non-biblical Jewish prayers written prior to 100 BC that ask God to guide people through temptations and evils. In a non-biblical book, the *Book of Jubilees*, probably written prior to 100 BC, we find prayers asking God to guide people through temptations and evils. For example, in a prayer of Noah from the *Book of Jubilees*, Noah asks God to protect his sons: "Let your grace be lifted up upon my sons, and do not let the evil spirits rule over them. . . . And let them not rule over the spirits of the living . . . and do not let them have power over the children of the righteous." Asking God to save or keep the supplicant from trial or temptation is a common theme in many Jewish prayers in early rabbinic literature as well as today. The second prayer that follows the *Shema*, the *Hashbikenu*, reads: "Drive away the evil one from before us and behind us."

Jewish Prayers That Resemble the Lord's Prayer

We've been examining parts of Jewish prayers and connecting them with elements of the *amidah* and Our Father. Now let's consider *whole* Jewish prayers that resemble the Lord's Prayer. Continuing to keep in mind the difficulties of dating Jewish prayers, let's look at some ancient examples.

First, here is a version of a Jewish prayer called the *Kaddish*. As I noted earlier, this prayer is prayed in parts of the liturgy of the synagogue, although in common parlance, the word *Kaddish* is used to refer to a particular prayer prayed by mourners at a funeral or after burial. This prayer from evening services for the

Sabbath and festivals almost reads like a shortened version of the Lord's Prayer:

> Magnified and sanctified be his great name in the world that he has created according to his will. May he establish his kingdom in your lifetime and in your days and in the lifetime of all the house of Israel, even speedily and at a near time.

Another form of the *Kaddish* prayer, called the "Half Kaddish," also resembles the Lord's Prayer:

> Exalted and hallowed be his great name in the world which he created according to his will. May he establish his kingdom . . . in your lifetime and in your days, and in the lifetime of the whole household of Israel, speedily and at a near time.

The Talmud tells Jews that during times of danger or emergency, when you cannot pray the full *amidah*, you're allowed to pray an abbreviated form of the prayer. Rabbis often taught such abbreviated versions to their students.[3] This abbreviated *amidah* used for the Sabbath reads: "Grant us relief for thou art our Father, and reign thou over us speedily, for thou art our King . . ."

Remember, Jesus was familiar with Jewish prayers of this kind. Consider this fact as you contemplate the scenes in the gospels of Mathew and Luke where Jesus asks his followers to pray the prayer we have come to know as the Our Father or Lord's Prayer.

There Are Two Versions of the Lord's Prayer in the Gospels

It is true: there are two settings or scenes where Jesus shares this prayer. In Matthew's gospel, the scene opens at the beginning of chapter 5 when Jesus begins a lengthy teaching of "the crowds" known as the Sermon on the Mount. This part of the gospel includes his presentation on the Beatitudes, teachings on the law, anger, adultery, divorce, and more. Early in chapter 6, Jesus begins a teaching on prayer. He offers instruction to "not be like the hypocrites, who love to stand and pray in the synagogues and street corners so that others may see them" (6:5). He says to "not babble like the pagans, who think that they will be heard because of their many words" (6:7). Perhaps, Jesus here is teaching like the rabbis, telling his Jewish crowd not to memorize their prayers, but to keep them spontaneous.

Jesus then introduces the prayer by simply saying, "This is how you are to pray." Note that Jesus does not tell the crowd, "Say this," or "Pray in these words." This is very consistent with what we've learned concerning Jewish traditions of prayer: that prayer should be spontaneous. It is risky to comment on what Jesus does *not* say, but it might be significant that Jesus is not telling the crowds the specific words to pray but giving a form to follow. He is telling them *how* to pray, not what words to recite.

The introduction to the text of the Lord's Prayer in Luke's gospel is simple: Jesus was praying alone in a "certain place, and when he had finished, one of his disciples said to him, 'Lord, teach us to pray just as John taught his disciples" (Lk 11:1). This certainly resembles the common practice of rabbinic figures teaching their students and followers particular, abbreviated versions of the *amidah*. Jesus then gives his disciples the prayer.

Then, without comment, Jesus continues to explain what their attitude to prayer ought to be. To do this, he uses the parable of the friend who comes at midnight to ask for bread for an unexpected visitor. I think it is noteworthy in the account from Luke 11:1–8 that there is no reaction by Jesus' disciples to the prayer that Jesus had just told them to pray! While, again, it is risky to argue from their silence, in my mind, I look at this scene and think that the reaction of the disciples is not noted because they may well have simply shrugged their shoulders when Jesus gave them the prayer. They may have been thinking, "Really? Is that it? The prayer you gave us is the prayer we already pray three times a day. We were hoping for something special. We've been praying that prayer since we were kids!" This is consistent, too, with the tone of Luke 11:9–13, which says that if an earthly father already knows how to respond to requests from his children, certainly our Father knows how to give us what we need. It seems Jesus is telling his disciples not to make such a big deal about particular words of a prayer—just pray as you have always prayed.

Putting It All Together!

We've studied the Lord's Prayer so carefully because it seems to me that understanding how Jesus wanted us to pray is very important. How we pray tells us a lot about how we think of God and how we think of ourselves in relation to God. It has been noted for centuries that the Our Father encapsulates much of what Jesus thought about God and what he wanted to teach his followers about God.

There is a very good possibility that this wonderful prayer that we Christians have been praying for two thousand years is a Jewish prayer, an abbreviated *amidah*. As such it was a prayer already known and prayed by Jesus and by his first followers. Jesus perhaps knew that his disciples were looking for something "special," some prayer that was extravagant, peculiar, or unique to him and his followers. But Jesus surprised them by telling them to just keep praying the prayer they already knew and had been praying three times a day their whole lives! Doing this tells us a lot about Jesus' religious belief and practice. It was a surprise to my mother to learn that Jesus was not an Irish Catholic! He wasn't. Jesus was a Jew. His thinking about God was shaped by his Jewish faith, the faith he learned from his parents and those around him. Recognizing Jesus' religious heritage in the Lord's Prayer, the prayer he asked us to pray, makes this so clear.

Why Is It Important to Understand What It Meant to "Sit at Table" in the Gospels?

This simple English phrase "sit at table" (and its variations) is another example of how a translator can rob us of the true meaning of a biblical text if it is not translated accurately. And like other words and phrases, the deeper meaning of this particular phrase will have implications for how we understand several scenes in the gospels.

The English translation of "sit at table" for a Greek phrase that is found in the gospels was a misappropriation of the way the phrase originally appeared in Greek. Remember, the period during which the New Testament was written and the culture from which it emerges was Hellenistic. Though the Romans were in power, Rome herself had become Hellenized years before. The Romans copied Greek architecture, sculpture, literature, and drama. Even the Greek language was embraced by educated Romans. The "cultured" Romans of the time spoke both Latin and Greek. Along with this embraced Hellenism in the Roman Empire came another cultural trapping from the Greeks: their table etiquette.

Greek Words for Table Etiquette in the New Testament

Ancient Romans in Jesus' day, like the Greeks, did not sit to eat. They *reclined* on couches to eat. Exactly why the Greeks initially began to take this posture to dine is a bit mysterious. Many believe it was a custom the Greeks took from the Persians, dating from the sixth century BC, but this is not certain. Anyone who has ever eaten from a reclined position can attest that it is not the most comfortable way to eat. So it is surprising that it became the norm among the Greeks and subsequently among the Romans too. But it did. So common had eating while reclining on couches become among the ancient Romans that the Latin word for dining room was *triclinium*—"the three-couch place."

In the New Testament, primarily the gospels, we have many scenes of banquets and meals. The Greek words used in the New Testament for the posture of the diners—to recline—are two synonyms: ανακειμαι *(anakeimai)*and ανακλινομαι *(anaklinomai)*. The word ανακειμαι is used fourteen times and the word ανακλινομαι occurs six times. Interestingly these two words are found *only* in the gospels. Here I should also note that the literal Greek word for "sit" does occur in the New Testament. In fact, there are two words for it too: καθιζω *(kathizō)* and καθημαι *(kathemai)*. These Greek words for "sit" are found throughout the New Testament and occur forty-six times and ninety-one times, respectively. However, neither of these two words ever occur in the New Testament to mean "sit" at a table for a meal. For eating, only ανακειμαι and ανακλινομαι—"to recline"—were used. In fact, so typical is this posture for dining in Hellenistic culture that the word for "dinner guest" in Greek is a participle form of either ανακειμαι or ανακλινομαι, meaning "one who reclines" or "the reclining one."

Imagining the Greek Dining Room

To fit the chosen posture for sharing a meal, the typical or traditional dining room was furnished with couches, generally arranged in a large U-formation, from the center of the room extending to couches butting up against the three walls of the dining room. Depending on the wealth of the host and the size of the dining room, the couches could be large enough to hold three or four guests each. It is said that the emperor Nero had over sixty large couches in his imperial *triclinium*. Diners would recline by leaning on their left elbows. They would reach for food from low-lying small tables placed in front of their couches with their right hands. (It was considered impolite for a person's left hand to come in contact with food.)

A dinner guest's position of honor and importance was marked by the geographical location of the couch in the dining room. This seems really weird to us. But at a Greek or Roman banquet, the farther away you were from the host during a meal, the less important you were. The closer you were to the host, the more honor you were being shown. Also, the person's position on the couch was significant too. On the central couch of the host, the person reclining nearest to him is more important than those reclining further away from the host on the couch. So think, for example, of the host's couch accommodating three diners. The guest reclining on the right side of the host, next to him, has his upper back against the host's chest. This is the position of the most honored guest.

The host of the dinner had the most prominent of all places. His couch was at the theoretical epicenter of the U-shape arrangement, and he was reclining on his left side on this couch. The degrees of honor moved out from that center couch, weakening as it "spread" throughout the dining room and moved toward the walls and the ends of the U-arrangement of the couches.

There are more peculiarities. Not only did your position in the dining room mark your level of honor, but even the menu of the meal changed as it moved out from the center, from the host's position. That meant that the guests within the first ring of couches could be eating the finest foods. For today's American diners, let's say the equivalent of filet mignon, steamed asparagus with béarnaise sauce, and twice-baked potatoes. The diners in the next ring out might be served fried chicken and French fries, and the guests in the ring farthest from the host might be eating oatmeal and warm water. All of these different food menus were in place for the same dinner!

Jesus and His Followers Reclined to Eat Too!

In the gospels, when we read about Jesus dining or telling a story about people dining, you should realize that he's referring to this style of dining. But in our modern English translations of the Bible, the two Greek words ανακειμαι and ανακλινομαι are rarely translated to mean "recline." Instead they are translated into English as "to sit." Why did the translators do this? And, a second question: What difference does it make?

Doubtlessly the Greek words for "recline" were translated into the English "sit" because in *our* English-speaking culture, sitting is the universal posture for dining. For me, the practice of translating this way raises many issues about the philosophy and guidelines for translating scripture, questions I won't deal with here. Suffice to say the translators were guided in their work by their consideration of, and focus on, the *target* audience, not the *original* audience of the biblical writer. In our culture we *sit* to eat, so when the scripture text is about eating, the translators had us in mind.

As to the second question—What difference does it make?— I'd say it makes a considerable difference. Translating one word or phrase incorrectly has a ripple effect and can easily contribute to problems in understanding other texts of the New Testament. Let me offer a couple of examples in which knowing how these people dined is of immense help in understanding the larger scriptural context as well as the intended message of Jesus.

Let's Look at the Parable of the Rich Man and Lazarus

In this parable, found only in the Gospel of Luke (16:19–31), Jesus tells of a very poor man, Lazarus, lying at the door of a rich man's house. Lazarus is longing for food, even yearning to eat the scraps that fall from the rich man's table. He is also ill and in such desperate straits that he has sores on his skin that dogs come to lick. For a Jewish audience, Jesus is painting a picture of a man not only desperately poor but also marked with extreme ritual impurity. In my mind there is at least one person in Jesus' audience who is disgusted to the point of nausea by the overly graphic depiction given by Jesus of this ritually unclean man. I can envision the person waving his hand at Jesus and saying, "For heaven's sake, we get it! He's unclean. Enough with the details! I just had my lunch and you're making me sick! Get on with the story!" Well, that's my fantasy anyway. But truly Jesus' description of Lazarus would have made any observant Jewish listener wince.

What does Jesus say about Lazarus? He tells the crowd that he died and went to heaven: "When the poor man died, he was carried away by angels to the bosom of Abraham" (Lk 16:22). This is a very interesting description, to say the least! Whenever I hear it, I am brought back to my fifth-grade class where our wonderful and very effective teacher, Sr. Maurelia, S.S.N.D., would read to us from the old *Benziger Brothers' Bible History* book every Friday afternoon. On one of those days, Sister read us this story of Lazarus. Of course, as typical ten-year-old boys, we all giggled at the mention of "Abraham's bosom." And, being the smart aleck that I was, I shot up my hand. "Sister, I have two questions about this story. Why does Abraham have a bosom and what is Lazarus doing on them?" As soon as I got the laughs I was after, Sister promptly put me in my place, told me I had to stay after school, and restored order. But seriously, ever since then I always thought that this was the strangest thing I'd ever heard from the Bible. It would be years before I was able to finally understand this scene.

You may have already figured out that the interpretation of this parable turns completely on the knowledge that these people ate from a reclined position. "Carried away to the bosom of Abraham" means that Lazarus is reclining on a couch with Abraham and therefore dining at a banquet. Lazarus is reclining on a couch with Abraham, leaning against his host, immediately to his left. This means Lazarus is reclining to the right of Abraham, the position of greatest honor at the heavenly meal!

Now back to Jesus' audience. As Jews were listening to this, they would have understood from Jesus' graphic description of the destitute Lazarus that he was a man of uber-uncleanness who would have been absolutely forbidden to share a meal with anyone. Lazarus's over-the-top ritual impurity (lying on the ground, having lesions on his skin, and especially having such intimate contact with dogs, which were ritually unclean animals) would have barred him from all gatherings of religious and polite society. Yet in Jesus' parable, Lazarus is not only sharing a meal; he's the guest of honor at a heavenly banquet given by our father Abraham! Truly UN-believable! So think for a moment of the probable reaction and thought process of Jesus' audience. In less than the two minutes it took to hear the entire parable, poor Lazarus has been catapulted from the absolute lowest person, ritually speaking, from abject poverty and ritual filth to the greatest honor imaginable—the guest of honor of Abraham at a heavenly banquet! It must have caused mental whiplash for Jesus' hearers!

But note, too, that Jesus doesn't have to explain or describe Lazarus' post-mortem status in any detail. With the simple phrase "to the bosom of Abraham," this "dining-while-reclining" audience immediately understood that the setting is a heavenly banquet and that Lazarus is the guest of honor.

There Are Other Gospel Examples to Consider

The Greek word used for Abraham's "bosom" is κολπος (*kolpos*), and it is also used in John 13:23. The scene is the Last Supper. "One of his disciples, the one whom Jesus loved, was reclining at Jesus' side." The Greek text in John 13:25 sounds even more intimate, because it states, he "leaned back against his κολπος." Here, too, knowing how they ate tells us an awful lot about how to interpret the text, far more than the simple translations. Not only does this passage reveal the intimacy of Jesus' friendship with the beloved disciple, but also it tells us that he is at the place of honor during this meal.

Another example to consider is a "mini-parable" describing the conduct of invited guests and hosts in Luke 14:7–14. In this example, Jesus uses this very notion of "honor" being determined by the geography of the dining room. In this brief admonition, Jesus is apparently at a banquet and he was "noticing how they (the guests) were choosing the places of honor at the table." So, he "told a parable to those who had been invited" (14:7). Then Jesus simply says, "When you are invited by someone to a wedding banquet, do not recline at table in the place of honor. A more distinguished guest than you may have been invited by him, and the host who invited both of you may approach you and say, 'Give your place to this man,' and then you would proceed with embarrassment to take the lowest place" (14:8–9). You can hear the host saying something like, "Hey you! Back to the couch where you belong! Over there where they're eating oatmeal!" Jesus goes on to say: "Rather when you are invited, go and take the lowest place so that when the host comes to you he may say, 'My friend, move up to a higher position.' Then you will enjoy the esteem of your companions at the table" (14:10).

Jesus also had instructions for the person hosting the meal: "When you hold a lunch or a dinner, do not invite your friends or your brothers or your relatives or your wealthy neighbors, in case they may invite you back and you have repayment. Rather, when you hold a banquet, invite the poor, the crippled, the lame, the blind [all ritually unclean and normally *un*-welcome at a meal, just like Lazarus from the story above!], blessed indeed will you be" (14:12–14). Your mental picture of this short parable has probably changed as you now imagine poor, ritually impure people exchanging places with the rich and affluent in the U-shape formation of couches arranged for this banquet.

Elsewhere, in Mark 12:38–39 (and its parallel in Luke 11:43) Jesus says: "Beware of the scribes, who like to go around in long robes and accept greetings in the marketplaces, seats of honor in synagogues, and *places of honor at banquets*" (Mk 12:38–39, emphasis mine). Note that the English phrase, "places of honor" in the text both in Mark and in Luke is the translation of the single Greek word: πρωτοκλισια, which literally means "the first dining couch" or "the first dining group."

A Proper Translation Is Crucial for Our Understanding of Scripture!

How rich is God's Word! The text of the Bible is fulfilling to any and all who read it, in whatever translation it is read. But I think we can see how important an accurate translation is of words and phrases from their original language to our own. Translating from one modern language to another is difficult enough, but translating ancient texts that emerged from cultural worlds that disappeared centuries ago adds a whole new challenge. Because these texts are the sacred, inspired Word of God, an even higher level of precision is needed.

None of this means that we all have to study Greek, Hebrew, and Aramaic in order to understand the Bible. I certainly do not intend to give the impression that the riches of reading the Bible are reserved to the few—the pinheads and professors like me! Not at all! At the same time, we must admit that we Catholics can certainly improve in educating ourselves about the Bible.

Let me give an example of what I mean. After guiding a group of parishioners through some scenes in the gospel described in this chapter concerning Hellenistic meals, I concluded and asked if there were any questions. One man raised his hand and shared with us that he was a cradle Catholic and had been active in his parish for over a decade. He said what I'd been teaching them over the previous two hours was completely new to him. He said, "Father, I've been a Catholic all my life and I've never heard any of the stuff you've been teaching us here." I replied, "Well I got here as fast as I could!"

Granted, my reply to that man in the audience was a bit snarky, but by that I meant to highlight the fact that while this material was new to *him*, none of it was a secret. This isn't information shared privately or intended for reading and research by only a few. No; Catholic authors have been writing wonderful books and articles about Catholic biblical study and biblical interpretation for decades. And most Catholics *are* literate! We can occasionally pick up a book about Bible study and read it ourselves! And many parishes have Bible study groups to help parishioners deepen and broaden their biblical literacy. If we are to be enriched deeply by God's Word, we should not leave it only to others to help us. It is not the job only of the priest or deacon to educate us about the surprising riches that are in store for those who take Bible study seriously.

The most wonderful part of studying biblical texts for me has always been the phenomenon of reading texts that are very

familiar to me and seeing them, understanding them, in surprisingly new and fresh ways. Learning about the background
and context of these familiar texts always reveals surprises to
me. And while my students will not always agree with me, for
me, this is the fun and the profound satisfaction that Bible study
always affords.

≺ 17 ≻

Is "Disciple" a Made-Up Word?

Before getting off the subject of words that translators had trouble moving from ancient languages like Greek and Hebrew to modern languages like English, we must take a look at another very important biblical word: *disciple*. Also, I'd like to point out that my own term that I mentioned earlier—*religification*, the packing of a biblical term with religious meaning—certainly applies to the term *disciple* and how it has come to be understood today.

Disciple is the English translation for the original Greek word used in the New Testament for both the followers of John the Baptist and the followers of Jesus. This Greek word, μαθητης (*mathetēs*), is found over two hundred times in the New Testament. However, when the word was used in the Greek language of Jesus' day, it had no particular religious significance. The Greek word μαθητης simply meant *student*. This term could have been used to describe a student of medicine, a student of dancing, a student of rhetoric or philosophy, or any other kind of student. Again, there was nothing "religious" in how it was used at all.

When the New Testament was translated into Latin, the ancient translator translated the simple Greek word μαθητης with the equally simple and equivalent Latin word for student, *discipulus*. This Latin word likewise had no particular religious connotation. It just meant *student*.

But when the English translator set to work translating the New Testament from the Latin, somehow it was thought that a follower of Jesus couldn't possibly be called just a plain student. Jesus' followers could not be called the same word used for a schoolboy in this view. So the Latin word for student *discipulus* was anglicized, or altered to make it look and sound more like an English word. So the typically Latin *-us* ending on the noun was removed and replaced with the more English looking *-ple* ending. *Voila!* Disciple was born!

Perhaps one can sympathize with the English translator for doing this; wishing to distinguish those first followers of Jesus as special, somehow too religious or holy to be known as "just a student." But the fact remains that the English word "disciple" is itself a made-up word for a very simple Greek word that means student.

How the Creation of the Word *Disciple* Affects Our Understanding of the Bible

Once again, you may be thinking, "So what? Regardless of its origins, disciple now *is* an English word and its meaning is crystal clear." True, but the translator is a robber! He robs us of the full meaning of the original words. By not translating the Greek word μαθητης as "student," we lose at least one important insight about the nature of Jesus and how he was perceived by his earliest contemporaries.

I'll bet you can easily guess which insight about the nature of Jesus I am referring to. The word *disciple* (or its plural form) occurs more than 250 times in the New Testament. Almost all these uses are references to the followers of Jesus. Now think for a moment. If Jesus' followers were repeatedly called his "students," then what does that tell us about what Jesus' contemporaries thought about Jesus? If you need more clues, ask yourself: Whom do students follow? Whom do students listen to? Right! A teacher!

If Jesus' followers were constantly called "students," then that tells us that those who knew and wrote about Jesus thought of him constantly as a teacher! Yet in our English translations, this insight (and I think it's an important insight)—that Jesus is a teacher—is not always available to us. Do note that on fifteen occasions in the gospels, Jesus is called "Rabbi," which literally means "my great one" and was a title that was used for teachers. So we do have some sense that Jesus is a teacher. But the translator of the Latin *discipulus* has robbed us of this significant aspect, that fuller appreciation of how Jesus was perceived by those who followed him and those who witnessed his life on earth.

Finally, and curiously, the mistranslation of disciple from Latin to English did not occur in all languages. For example, the German word for "disciple" is *Schüler*. This is also the German word for "student." So German translations of the New Testament preserve this notion about Jesus being understood to have been a teacher.

In this case, the translator who "robbed" us of a proper understanding of an important biblical term was an Englishman!

What Do You Mean There Is No Holy Spirit in the Bible?

The term *holy spirit*, most often written in English with capital letters—Holy Spirit—is another perfect example of how translators have hidden some important aspects of a term's meaning. Holy Spirit (with capital letters) is a very central term in Christian belief. The Holy Spirit is the third divine person of the Blessed Trinity. The Holy Spirit is God.

But to fully examine what this term meant to original biblical audiences, we have to reach way back into Old Testament texts and to the anthropology of that ancient world. Let's start by looking at each of the two words. This phrase in Hebrew, *ruah YHWH*, literally means "YHWH's breath." Note also that in Hebrew, the phrase is transposed: *ruah* stands for "spirit"; YHWH of course stands for God and is the sacred, personal name for God that the second commandment forbade Jews to pronounce. Translators, prohibited from using the sacred name, often replaced it with the euphemism "holy." I'll return to this part of the phrase later. Let's first look at that word *ruah*.

Understanding the Meaning
of *Ruah*

This Hebrew word *ruah* originally meant wind. *Ruah* is used to describe wind dozens of times in the Old Testament. In Genesis 8:1, "God made a wind sweep over the earth." In Psalm 1:4, the wicked "are like chaff driven by the wind." In Isaiah 57:13, the wind will destroy false idols: "All these the wind shall carry off, a mere breath shall bear them away." There are many other instances in the Old Testament (e.g., Ps 103:16, Is 41:16, Ez 3:12–14) where the word *ruah* simply means "wind" or "breeze."

But, as indicated in the passage from Isaiah above, the word for wind also means breath—the air that goes in and out of the mouths and noses of humans and animals. We must remember that while we think of these ancient people as prescientific, they were keen observers of the natural world. And one can see, by extension, how the word for wind could also mean breath. Think of how both the wind and your breath can blow out the flame of a match.

Why Is God's Name Connected
with Ruah?

While we now have an orientation that the Hebrew *ruah* means wind or breath and is translated to the English *spirit*, we must wonder why God's name—YHWH—is connected to this phrase. The answer is a simple one: there was a common and profound belief of ancient Jews that the breath that goes in and out of the lungs of human beings and animals—the "wind" that gives them life—is not just some random moving air, but in fact is the very breath of God. Where did this idea come from?

Let's look at the creation story in Genesis for help. In Genesis 1:2 we read of "a mighty wind sweeping over the waters" as God created the heavens and the earth. The Hebrew words in this passage are *ruah Elohim* (the "breath of God"). Elohim is a Hebrew word for God. Genesis 2:7 includes a synonym for this phrase to describe how God created the first human being: "the LORD God formed the man out of the dust of the ground and blew into his nostrils the breath of life." It was God's breath that brought life to this random collection of "dust of the ground." Genesis 7:15 and 22, describing the great flood, explain that same breath of God is shared by both human beings and all animals; for example: "Pairs of all creatures in which there was the breath of life came to Noah into the ark. . . . Everything on dry land with the breath of life in its nostrils died." Both humans and animals live by breathing in and out the breath of God—*ruah Yahweh*. This wind was breathed into the first human being and is breathed into all living creatures by God himself; it is what makes them live.

The ancients believed that all creatures were breathing God's breath in and out of their lungs. But they also knew that while God's breath gave life to creatures, the bodies of both humans and animals seemed to have life not only in the whole, but also in their individual parts. They saw that somehow the parts of living creatures—hands, feet, ears, elbows, knees, and more—were *also* living parts. And being keen observers, they asked themselves how this life-giving breath of God actually spreads to all the individual parts of the body.

Today, through science, we understand that when we breathe in oxygen, it is taken into our lungs and then is absorbed into our bloodstream. We likewise understand that when we breathe out, carbon dioxide is drawn out of the blood and into the lungs and then exhaled. The ancient people didn't have the benefits of modern science. They wondered how this wind, this breath of God, penetrates through the "meat" of the body—the muscles, bones, tissues, and bodily extremities—after it enters the mouth and the nose.

To answer this question, they considered their experiences of slaughtering an animal. They noted that when the windpipe and the two major blood vessels on either side of the windpipe were cut, blood came out of the animal—a *lot* of blood. The breathing stopped, and the animal died. They knew that this was also true for a person (see Baruch 2:17). From their observations, they drew the conclusion that the breath of God being drawn in through the nose and mouth then went down through the windpipe or throat. They concluded that it must be in the throat that this breath of God gets absorbed by the blood flowing through the two large blood vessels on either side of the throat. From there, filled with God's life-giving breath, they understood that the breath was carried by the blood to all the parts of the body.

They knew that no matter where you cut or pricked the skin of animals or humans, blood would flow. Because of this, they understood that God's living breath was distributed by the blood throughout every possible place in the bodies of both animals and humans. What we now know happens in the lungs—the absorption of oxygen into the blood—they thought happened in the throat. This is probably why the Hebrew word for throat—*nephesh*—also came to mean "soul," that is, the living core of a person.

This understanding also helps to explain why blood—whether of animals or of persons—was filled with ritual taboos for ancient Judaism. Their laws concerning the treatment of blood are very specific and filled with sanctions. One could not touch and certainly could not consume blood. It was too sacred because it bore the very breath of God in it. After an animal was butchered—whether in a sacred way in the Temple or simply in a butcher shop—all of the blood had to be *completely* drained from the carcass before an observant Jew could eat the meat. And the blood in either situation could not be drained into a sewer. It had to drain directly into the earth. All of these ritual practices were in place because of the Jewish belief that blood contains the life-giving breath of God within it.

The Holy Spirit in the New Testament

Let's look at some of the implications of how the understanding of *ruah YHWH*—holy spirit—in the Old Testament showed up in the New Testament. In the New Testament, the phrase "holy Spirit" is found over ninety times. In Greek the word for "spirit"— πνευμα (*pneuma*) or πνοη (*pnoe*)—has the same ambiguity that *ruah* has in Hebrew. The word means both "wind" and "breath." Whereas the ancient Hebrew writers had used the sacred name of God—*YHWH*—Greek translators, to avoid even coming close to breaking the second commandment, replaced the sacred name simply with the word "holy" (αγιος in Greek). The complete Greek translation of "holy spirit" in the New Testament is πνευμα αγιον.

As we've noted before, ancient Greek manuscripts of the New Testament have no punctuation, no capital letters, no commas, and no periods (see chapter 8). You will never find capital letters in the phrase "holy spirit" in any ancient biblical text. This may not seem all that significant till you consider the difference between "Holy Spirit" and the "holy spirit"—the first with capital letters and the second without. And remember the original readers of the text would understand the phrase as something like "holy breath." Needless to say, this is a different understanding of how Christians understand the capitalized phrase today. The understanding of the Holy Spirit as the Third Person of the Holy Trinity would not be fully defined until some centuries after the New Testament was written. So when we read the New Testament, we should not impose the capital letters and our definition of Holy Spirit on the phrase, but think of holy spirit as the first Greek speakers and hearers would have understood it: as the "breath of God." Hence, to answer the question that heads up this chapter, technically the Holy Spirit (with capital letters and to define the Third Person of the Trinity) does not appear in the Bible!

Reading "Holy Spirit" in a New Way

If we imagine the phrase "holy Spirit" in the way it was originally intended by the biblical writers, as the "breath of God," then we can gain some profound insights about what the phrase reveals about the beliefs of our ancestors in the faith. For example, let's look at the appearance of risen Jesus to his disciples on the first day of the week in the locked upper room from John 20:19–22. In this scene Jesus greets them saying, "Peace be with you." Then Jesus tells his disciples (students), "As the Father has sent me, so I send you." When he said this, he breathed on them. Then he said, "Receive the holy Spirit."

Think about these gathered disciples, the frightened, hiding early Church. I imagine that these followers of Jesus, due to their Jewish background, understood Jesus' breathing on them was related to that scene from Genesis of God breathing life into the lifeless clay of the first human being or God's breath hovering over the lifeless chaotic water before creation. Now, after Jesus' death and Resurrection, the disciples experience that Jesus is alive and is sharing new life with them. He breathes his new divine life into them.

Next, focus on another later, familiar scene in the Acts of the Apostles (2:1–41). The same frightened followers of Jesus are gathered again in the upper room, this time on the day of Pentecost, and a "strong driving wind, . . . filled the entire house in which they were. Then there appeared to them tongues as of fire, which parted and came to rest on each one of them" (2:2–3). Note not only the mention of wind but the presence of flames of fire as graphic proof of the presence of the wind. (While wind can be felt, it can't be seen, but *evidence* of it can be seen in something like a flickering flame or swirling smoke.)

Most importantly, after this in-blowing of the wind that filled the upper room, the disciples seem to take on new life: "And they were all filled with the holy Spirit" (2:4). Thereafter, we see them no longer cowering behind locked doors but boldly preaching before a large crowd gathered from all over the Mediterranean for the Pentecost feast. Filled with new life—the breath of God given to them by the risen Jesus—the followers of Jesus, the early Church, come alive.

Finally, with our new knowledge of *ruah* meaning wind or breath, let's return briefly to the subject of ancient baptism, discussed in chapter 12. In the early Church, baptism was a secret rite. Christians were forbidden from revealing any description of it to the non-baptized. Imagine the person about to be baptized, who knew nothing of the rite he or she was about to undergo. The hand of the baptizer pushes the person's head down into the water three times! Not knowing what is going on, it is easy to imagine the person in a panic and that once allowed to raise his or her head up out of the water, the person would be gasping for air, literally pulling breath into the lungs. The newly baptized person was breathing in the *ruah*, the breath of life. Can you hear the three loud gasps each time the person's head comes up out of the water? Can you see in this rite of baptism a repeat of the encounter the disciples in the upper room had with the risen Lord, when he breathed new life into them? A new Christian dies in the waters of baptism, but is given new life "in the name of the Father and of the Son and of the Holy Spirit" by three times taking in the breath of God.

A Final Word on God's Love and Studying Sacred Scripture

Earlier in this book, I compared the discovery of the hand of God working in my life at the time of my parents' deaths with the theological reflection undertaken by the People of God that would ultimately produce the sacred scriptures. God's acting in my life had been invisible to me as I struggled with grief and loss. In the aftermath of my parents' deaths, I could not see God working in my life. Quite the contrary, I felt abandoned by God. It was only later that my own barrier of invisibility was lifted. It was then that I discovered that God *had* been working on my behalf during that time of grief and sadness. I just couldn't see it at the time.

In the years since—and fueled by recognizing more of the depth of God's love for us through my study of scripture—I've come to learn that this is a typical way that God acts in our lives. The evidence of God's love and the evidence of the kingdom of God are all around us. So much of it is visible, perceivable by those "who have eyes to see." And don't we all have times in our lives when we can recognize God's presence in our own lives and in the larger world?

We recognize God's love in the beauty of nature and are in awe. We look at the love and sacrifice made for us by people we know well (like my cousin Nancy Kay made for me in preparing a family photo album) and people we don't know at all (like the driver who let me cut in on the crowded Dan Ryan Expressway). We appreciate it when these insights come clearly to us. We also begin to understand that all of these rich gifts are only a miniscule reflection of the richness of God's love.

However, most often we are too concerned with the demands of daily life to even think about such things, much less notice God acting all around us. And there are times when these miracles of God's love for us are so commonplace that we forget where they come from, if we recognize them at all. It is rare that we have any wonder about the tiny seed that produces a giant tree. We don't think twice about the loving ingenuity of our Creator.

Worse, when life is difficult and we feel beaten down by its demands and sorrows, we doubt that God's love even exists. We see no evidence of the kingdom of God in our own lives, much less in the world at large. Some people live their whole lives cynically depleted of wonder. They become jaded and live in stony blindness. For so many reasons, God's love is often invisible to us.

Jesus taught that God never stops loving us, even when we don't see it. It makes no difference to God whether our blindness is voluntary or the result of slow-growing cataracts brought on by terrible, desperate suffering. God's love for us continues anyway. There was a Latin inscription over the cave of the ancient oracle at Delphi in Greece. It was placed so that folks coming to consult the gods could easily read it: *Vocatus atque non vocatus, deus aderit,* that is, "Called or not, the god attends." Perhaps a similar Christian sign would read: *Vocatus atque non vocatus, Deus amat,* "Called or not, God loves." Whether we are aware of it or not, God loves us. This world and we who live in it are swimming in the love of God.

But what Jesus taught two thousand years ago was not just a theology class *about* God. He always added a challenge to his message that God loves us. Jesus didn't just tell a scholar of the law who questioned what was necessary for eternal life prior to the telling of the parable of the good Samaritan; he added an instruction. Like the Samaritan who went out of his way to care for and love an injured "enemy" on the side of the road, he told the scholar that he must "Go and do likewise" (Lk 10:37). Jesus challenges us to do the very same thing: to love others as God loves us. Is this not the message of the whole gospel? Is this not the nature of the kingdom of God that Jesus proclaimed? Is this not all of the revelation of God through the ages of history and the pages of the Bible summed up in one divine directive? Go and do likewise.

The rich sacred scriptures that the Church preaches and preserves through her many generations are not meant only as a *description* of God or his kingdom, but rather they are a call to action for us to be coworkers with God in order to assist him in building up the kingdom. When we love as God has first loved us, we bring the kingdom into more recognizable visibility. The kingdom of God becomes an ongoing epiphany revealing that God is always with us, made present and visible in every action of kindness and compassion.

While much concerning biblical study can be difficult, technical, and complex, it really is not all that complicated. When I find myself getting lost in my study and research of the Bible, I am brought back to the simple reality and challenge of Jesus' words to the scholar of the law: "Go and do likewise." Or, I hear the words of Mary to the waiters at the wedding in Cana: "Do whatever he tells you."

Notes

3. How Does the Church Study the Bible?

1. David A. Lysik, ed., *The Bible Documents: A Parish Resource with Commentary and Index* (Chicago, IL: Liturgy Training Publications, 2001).

2. Daniel J. Harrington, S.J., ed., *Witnesses to the Word: New Testament Studies since Vatican II* (Mahwah, NJ: Paulist Press, 2012).

4. What Are the Tools for Scripture Scholarship?

1. The Pontifical Biblical Commission, *The Interpretation of the Bible in the Church* (Boston: Pauline Books & Media, 1996), Part 1, Section A. Emphasis mine.

8. How Were Ancient Bibles Produced?

1. Bruce Metzger, *The Text of the New Testament: Its Transmission, Corruption, and Restoration,* 2nd ed. (New York: Oxford University Press, 1968), 15.

2. Metzger, *The Text of the New Testament,* 15.

11. Where Did Jesus Come From?

1. Joseph Ratzinger, *Jesus of Nazareth: The Infancy Narratives,* trans. Philip J. Whitmore (New York: Image, 2012), 61.

2. John P. Meier, *A Marginal Jew: Rethinking the Historical Jesus, Volume One: The Roots of the Problem and the Person* (New York: Anchor, 1991), 212.

3. Raymond E. Brown, *The Birth of the Messiah: A Commentary on the Infancy Narratives in the Gospels of Matthew and Luke,* updated edition (New York: Anchor, 1993), 171–173.

4. The great Catholic biblical scholar Fr. Raymond Brown disagrees with this point with regard to Luke. "It is more plausible that he (Luke) composes the [infancy] narrative from beginning to end himself, depending on some items of historical information and popular tradition, weaving in motifs and characterizations brought forward from the Old Testament and back from the Gospel" (Brown, *The Birth of the Messiah*, 498).

5. Raymond E. Brown, "Infancy Narratives in the NT Gospels," in David Noel Freedman, ed., *The Anchor Bible Dictionary,* vol. 3 (New York: Doubleday, 1992), 413–414.

13. Why Doesn't *Abba* Mean "Daddy"?

1. Thanks to James Barr for suggesting the title of this book in his two essays "Abba isn't daddy" (*JTS* 39, 1, 1988) and "'Abba, Father' and the Familiarity of Jesus' Speech" (*Theology*, 91, 1988).

15. What Are the Origins of the Lord's Prayer?

1. J. H. Charlesworth, "A Prolegomenon to a New Study of the Jewish Background of the Hymns and Prayers in the New Testament," *Journal of Jewish Studies* 33 (1982), 265–301.

2. *bShab* 151b.

3. D. Bivin, "Prayers for Emergencies," *Jerusalem Perspective* 5, 1992, 16–17.

Rev. William L. Burton, O.F.M., is a scripture scholar. He also serves as a provincial councilor for the Franciscan Province of the Sacred Heart.

He was a member of the board of trustees of the Catholic Theological Union and served stints as vice president for mission and ministry, vice president of academic affairs, and a professor at Quincy University. Burton also was director of academic formation for the diaconate program in the Diocese of Springfield and a visiting professor at DePaul University. A regular speaker at the Los Angeles Religious Education Conference and other venues, Burton has been involved in numerous parish Bible study programs and scripture-based retreats in the United States, Canada, and Rome. He has also served as a frequent pilgrimage guide through the Holy Land, Greece, and Turkey.

AVE

AVE MARIA PRESS

Founded in 1865, Ave Maria Press,
a ministry of the Congregation of
Holy Cross, is a Catholic publishing
company that serves the spiritual and
formative needs of the Church and its
schools, institutions, and ministers;
Christian individuals and families; and
others seeking spiritual nourishment.

For a complete listing of titles from

Ave Maria Press

Sorin Books

Forest of Peace

Christian Classics

visit avemariapress.com